Landscapes of
CORFU

a countryside guide
Eighth edition

Noel Rochford
revised by Sunflower Books

SUNFLOWER BOOKS

Eighth edition © 2017
Sunflower Books™
PO Box 36160
London SW7 3WS, UK
www.sunflowerbooks.co.uk

ISBN 978-1-85691-492-5

Pollarded Judas tree

Important note to the reader

We have tried to ensure that the descriptions and maps in this book are error-free at press date. It will be very helpful for us to receive your comments (sent to info@sunflowerbooks.co.uk, please) for the updating of future printings.

We also rely on those who use this book — especially walkers — to take along a good supply of common sense when they explore. Conditions change regularly between updatings of the book, and *storm damage or bulldozing may make a route unsafe at any time*. If the route is not as we outline it here, and your way ahead is not secure, return to the point of departure. *Never attempt to complete a tour or walk under hazardous conditions!* Please read the notes on pages 33-42 carefully, as well as the introductory comments at the beginning of each tour and walk (regarding road conditions, equipment, grade, distances and time, etc). Explore *safely*, while at the same time respecting the beauty of the countryside.

Cover photograph: Logas or 'Sunset' Beach at Peroulades
Title page: the 'view par excellence' over Cape Drastis

Photographs by the author, with the exception of pages 26 (bottom right), 47, 60-1, 62, 73, 81, 93, 100, 113, 119 (Mike Longridge); 2, 18, 20, 26 (left), 48, 50 (both), 51 (top right), 61 (right), 72, 86 (right), 110, 115, 116, 123 (bottom) (Robert Lefever); 12-13, 15, 22, 24, 25, 26 (top right), 28-9, 37, 40, 71, 83 (top), 86 (left), 90, 101 and the cover (Shutterstock)
Maps: Nick Hill for Sunflower Books. Base map data © OpenStreetMap contributors. Contour data made available under ODbL (opendata commons.org/licenses/odbl/1.0)
Drawings by Sharon Rochford
A CIP catalogue record for this book is available from the British Library.
Printed and bound in England: Short Run Press, Exeter

Contents

4 Landscapes of Corfu

Preface

For centuries Corfu's magnetic beauty has attracted travellers, who have sung the praises of the peacock-hued bays, the hillsides drenched in silvery-green olive trees, and the emerald greenness of the countryside. And when you leave Corfu, these will be your impressions too. While time brings change, the pristine Corfu so beloved of Lear and the Durrell brothers can still be found, and this book tells you where. It turns the island inside-out and helps you find a Corfu unknown to most tourists.

The book focuses on walking, but it is not intended *only* for walkers. The car touring section will show you the best of the island, and the picnic suggestions make an excellent introduction to the countryside — many of them being at exhilarating viewpoints, reached after only a very short, leg-stretching walk from your touring route. You just might be tempted to return another day and explore a bit further.

Walking on Corfu is sheer bliss. You will be spoilt by a kaleidoscope of landscapes, and you needn't be an intrepid hiker to find these beauty spots. The walks lead to some of the most beautiful beaches you'll ever see, from the secluded pebbly coves of the northwest to the pellucid horseshoe bay of Ag Georgios, the sand dunes of the Korission Lagoon and Durrell's favourite, Mirtiotissa. If you're adventurous, the rugged goat country of Mount Pantokrator will appeal to you. For strolls and short rambles, meander over the silvan hills or cross vast grassy plains flecked with flowers, surprise terrapin sunbasking in muddy ponds, plough through Corfu's few remaining holly oak woods, step across silently-flowing streams, and — in the bleaker corners of the island — listen to the echoes of abandoned villages.

In spring and autumn Corfu is at its best — alight with a spectacle of wild flowers that cover the colour spectrum. The fields and slopes are splashed with violet-blue Venus' looking-glass, flesh-pink geraniums, mauve anemones, vivid yellow marigolds, carmine cyclamen, creamy crocuses, sunflower-yellow *Sternbergia,* and elaborately-marked orchids. Even the thistles contribute to this floral splendour. And for fun, there's the squirting cucumber — touch it and see what happens!

Trees are another part of this finely-embroidered land-

5

scape. Perhaps the most eye-catching is the Judas tree in spring, with its dangling clusters of purple florets. In the country, massive oaks and twirling turpentine trees shade solitary dwellings and churches. Everywhere, the dark spires of the cypress pierce the island's cloak of olives.

Corfu has suffered a turbulent history of occupations and invasions — most recently the invasion of tourists. For four months of the year, the island is besieged by great hordes of them. This is the side of Corfu that you *don't* want to see. To know Corfu is to know the people. Out in the country is where you're more likely to experience the real friendliness — provided that *you* make the first move. So if you speak a smattering of Greek, don't hesitate to do so. The rewards will be immense. This is the Corfu of Lear and the Durrells. Taste the untainted rawness in the country, and not the synthetic spillage that follows tourism everywhere. There are today two Corfus and, with the help of *Landscapes of Corfu*, I hope you find the real island.

— NOEL ROCHFORD

Acknowledgements
Many thanks to people who have checked the walks and helped with updating over the years, especially Mike Longridge, David Baker, and the team at Sunflower Books.

Books and maps
Landscapes of Corfu is a *countryside guide* and should be used in tandem with a good standard guide, of which there are several available.

As a **field guide to the island's flora** I have used Huxley and Taylor, *Flowers of Greece and the Aegean* (Hogarth Press, 1989) and three books by George Sfikas (available on Corfu and possibly from Amazon or your usual supplier): *Wild Flowers of Greece, Trees and Shrubs of Greece,* and *Medicinal Plants of Greece.*

For information about the **Corfu Trail** and accompanying guide, see page 34.

Should you want another **map of Corfu** in addition to the detailed and handy 1:50,000 maps in this book, sheet maps are published by Freytag + Berndt (1:50,000) and Discovery Walking Guides (1:40,000).

If you've enjoyed Corfu, you may want to explore **other Ionian islands** using Sunflower guides:

Landscapes of Paxos by Noel Rochford features one car tour and many walks, all highlighted on a single sheet map (scale 1:28,000).

Walk & Eat Kefalonia by Brian and Eileen Anderson describes 10 walks and two excursions, all with restaurants en route — including their menus, local specialities and even recipes.

Zakynthos by Gail Schofield is a general guide covering everything from history to hotels but, in the Sunflower tradition, it emphasises the island's flora, wildlife and culture; the many walks and excursions are illustrated with both hand-drawn 3D and GPS-compatible maps.

Finally, for **background reading**, seek out the latest paperback editions of Lawrence Durrell's *Prospero's Cell* and Gerald Durrell's *My Family and Other Animals.*

Getting about

The two most popular and affordable ways of getting about on Corfu are by bus and rented transport. Even though the bus network is fairly extensive, it's not always convenient for walks and picnics. During peak season the buses are jam-packed and so sometimes do not call at intermediate bus stops, as they cannot take on any more passengers. And they often run late. For these reasons, *renting a vehicle is a good option*. Both circular walks and linear routes which can be done by using a car or bike in tandem with the buses are indicated in the Contents by the symbol 🚗. Often it is a short or alternative version of a walk which lends itself to this approach.

Car hire on the island is fairly expensive in high season, but less costly if you book and pay in advance, either with your tour operator or one of the lower-priced international car hire firms with agents on the island. **Scooter** and **bike rental**, however, is very economical all year round and two of the most popular ways of getting about.

Coach excursions allow you to see all the major sights in comfort, but they provide no opportunity for contact with countryside life. **Taxis** are another alternative, and sharing with others will help cut costs. Always agree on a price before setting out, and don't be afraid to do a little good-natured bargaining.

Those who prefer to use public transport should note that outside the main tourist resorts, the **local bus** network* (see timetables pages 128-134) serves the local populace, not the visitor. This means that buses leave Corfu Town for far-flung villages very early in the morning and return mid-afternoon. Some of the walks described end along these country bus routes. To catch the day's only return bus means galloping through some walks — not everyone's idea of a pleasant hike. The problem is exaggerated as the season tails off, when late afternoon buses from some resorts are discontinued. One way to overcome this problem is to stay overnight where your walk ends, which is not difficult outside July/August, since there are rooms for rent all over the island. Otherwise, you will have to arrange for friends or a taxi to collect you.

*See notes about buses and bus stations in the timetables on page 128; bus stations are shown on the town plan overleaf.

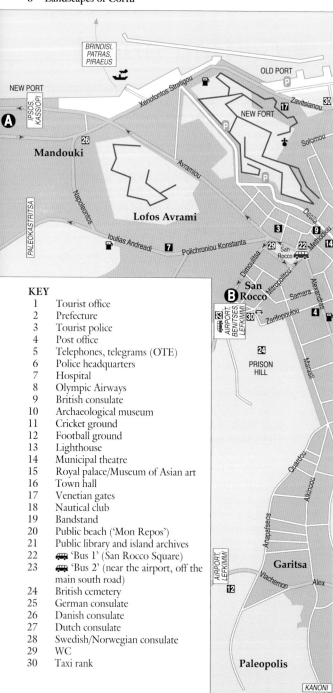

KEY

1   Tourist office
2   Prefecture
3   Tourist police
4   Post office
5   Telephones, telegrams (OTE)
6   Police headquarters
7   Hospital
8   Olympic Airways
9   British consulate
10 Archaeological museum
11 Cricket ground
12 Football ground
13 Lighthouse
14 Municipal theatre
15 Royal palace/Museum of Asian art
16 Town hall
17 Venetian gates
18 Nautical club
19 Bandstand
20 Public beach ('Mon Repos')
21 Public library and island archives
22 🚍 'Bus 1' (San Rocco Square)
23 🚍 'Bus 2' (near the airport, off the
    main south road)
24 British cemetery
25 German consulate
26 Danish consulate
27 Dutch consulate
28 Swedish/Norwegian consulate
29 WC
30 Taxi rank

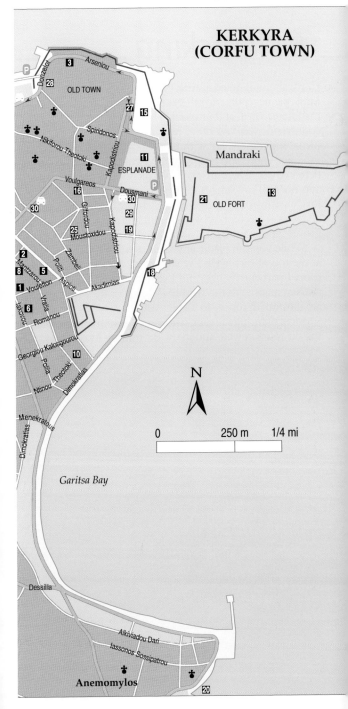

KERKYRA
(CORFU TOWN)

Picnicking

Corfu abounds in scenic little corners, many of which make ideal picnic spots. Ideal because they're far from the madding crowd, and unspoilt. They give you a feel for the countryside, yet you don't have to hike for miles. All my picnic suggestions are within easy reach, and most can be extended into short walks, should your curiosity get the better of you. There are no public picnic sites on the island, and none of my suggestions offers anything more than a lovely setting or a superb view. There are landscapes to suit all tastes — secluded coves, mountaintops, lagoons, olive groves, grassy fields, and abandoned monasteries.

While you can picnic anywhere along a walking route, at the top of each walk I've suggested one or more picnic spots I particularly like, and I've highlighted them on the *walking* maps with the symbol **P**. Many of the picnic spots are illustrated, too — to inspire you!

Most of my picnic suggestions are easily accessible from the car tours as well, and in the car touring introduction I

suggest that you refer to these large-scale maps from time to time. A few picnics, due to their isolation, require a short walk from the nearest parking place; if so, you will find all the information about how to get there in the notes for the relevant walk. Please remember that if more than a few minutes' walking is required, you will need to wear sensible shoes and to take a sunhat (some picnic spots are in full sun). Beach towels come in handy on sand or prickly terrain — maybe with something waterproof underneath early in the season when the ground might still be damp.

Of course you needn't be a picnicker to enjoy my suggestions; they make perfect 'leg stretchers' — a good way to break up a tour and visit places the casual tourist never sees. But if you *are* going to have a picnic, make it one to remember! Here's a short recipe for a healthy picnic: fresh fruit from the market, *angouria* (cucumbers), *domades* (tomatoes), a slab of *feta* (cheese), *mortadella* (a garlicky sausage), some *taramasalata* and *tzatziki* from the supermarket, some fleshy maroon olives (if you're into olives). Then pick up a loaf or two of fresh village bread en route. If you have a sweet tooth, add *baklava* (a pastry filled with nuts and oozing honey) or *rizogala* (cold rice pudding). Don't forget the wine!

You have various choices for a picnic from Afionas. The nearest spot is just four minutes away: take the wide alley (shown on page 83) opposite the front door of the church. Up amidst the white-washed houses, take the second alley on the left, followed by a right and then another left (all are signed to a restaurant). This path follows the spine of the ridge to seats looking out to Cape Ag Stefanos and Gravia Island. I call this the 'donkey parking lot': there are sometimes a few donkeys here, munching straw — it makes a terrific photo. Continue on the path down towards 'Porto/Double Bay', then ascend the hillock over to the right to Waypoint (3) — and enjoy this splendid view over the twin coves of Port Timone. You'll have this same view if you do Walk 14a and fork right at Waypoint (2) on the short path to Waypoint (3).

❀ Touring

Most tourists rent some form of transport for part, if not all, of their visit. **Car hire** is inexpensive out of the main season (April to October). It is preferable to stay with the well-known hire companies, through whom you can arrange and pay for hire before you leave, including all taxes, CDW, and unlimited mileage. There are also very reasonable fly-drive offers.

Take care when renting; check the car and take time to study the **rental conditions/insurance coverage**. It is imperative to ensure that 'collision damage waiver' is included in the insurance, to cover damage to your hire car if repair costs cannot be recovered from a third party. Tyre and windscreen damage (including punctures) are the responsibility of the hirer, so check carefully before you drive off, including the spare. Always carry the agency's phone number with you, and take some water, food, and warm clothing in case of breakdown.

Motorbikes and **mopeds** are very good value. *But beware when renting:* many are not serviced regularly, and breakdowns are frequent. Note also that during the high season youngsters pour onto Corfu. All rent mopeds and

The beautiful setting of the Paleokastritsa Monastery, the jewel of Liapades Bay, is best seen from this viewpoint just west of Lakones (Car tour 3). As you drive through Lakones you'll encounter traffic lights: roads in many of the villages are only wide enough for one car. Be patient: unless you are travelling one of the very few trunk roads, progress will be very slow. The combination of an unusually harsh winter in 2016/17 and the unhealthy economic climate means that almost all roads were in poor condition as we went to press — heavily patched and with very deep potholes. Bear in mind, too, that even when a road is shown as surfaced on our maps (and others), it may be very narrow and not built up at the edge — and it may suddenly lose its surface for several hundred metres. Expect the unexpected!

motorbikes, many for the first time. The accident rate is appallingly high. Drive slowly and attentively.

The touring notes are brief: they include little history or information about the towns — all this will be in your standard guide book (or freely available from the tourist offices). Instead, I've concentrated on the 'logistics' of touring: times and distances, road conditions, and seeing parts of the island that many tourists miss. Most of all, I emphasise possibilities for **walking** and **picnicking**. While some of my suggestions may not be suitable during a long car tour, you may see a landscape that you would like to explore at leisure another day.

The fold-out touring map is ideal for planning and compact while motoring. It contains all the information you will need outside Corfu Town. But note that most of the island has been mapped out at 1:50,000 for the walks: you may wish to refer to some of these detailed large-scale walking maps from time to time while touring.

The tours have been written up with Corfu Town (plan pages 8-9) as departure/return point: most of the major resorts are within easy reach of the capital. **Tours 1 and 3 should be given preference if time is limited.** The touring notes *include* time for visits. **Symbols** in the text correspond to those on the touring map; see the key.

All motorists should read the Country code on page 39 and go quietly in the countryside. *Kalo taxidi!*

Car tour 1: CORFU'S RIVIERA AND PANTOKRATOR

Corfu • Nissaki • Kassiopi • Ano Perithia • Acharavi • Episkepsis • Mt Pantokrator • Spartilas • Corfu

124km/77mi; 5-6 hours; Exit A from Corfu Town (plan pages 8-9)
Walks en route: 1-9, 11 (Alternative 3), 23
Picnic suggestions: All the walks listed above feature picnic spots shown by the symbol *P* on the relevant walking maps.

Opening hours
Ag Merkourios Chapel (Ag Markos): make arrangements at the archaeological museum in Corfu Town
Danilia Folklore Village (near Gouvia): 10.00-13.00, 18.00-22.00 daily except Sundays

T his drive is the most rewarding on the island. Circling the sprawling rocky mass of Pantokrator, you pass Corfu's Riviera — an unrivalled stretch of coastline etched with idyllic coves. Olive groves, splashed with cypress trees, forest the cascading hills. Ascending to Pantokrator, the landscape becomes harsher. You climb into scrubby hills laced with rocky outcrops. A plateau, strewn with mounds of rock, leads you to the tiny mountain peak, from where you can see every corner of the island and over to the tantalising mountains of Albania. Heading home under a mellow sun, you coil your way down to Ipsos Bay and a picture-postcard seascape.

Setting out from Corfu Town (Exit A), stay on the seafront, passing the old and new ports. When you reach the main north road at a T-junction (🅿), keep right. The first 16km of this tour follows Corfu's tourist strip — a haphazardly-built-up stretch of unexciting coastline. But the bold presence of Pantokrator and the pretty offshore islands of Lazaretto and Vidos are some compensation — as is the dual carriageway!
Kontokali (6.5km 🏨🏠✕🅿△) is the first of the tourist villages; fortunately, the dual carriageway bypasses all of these resorts. The road to the Danilia folklore village★ forks left at the large green Diella's Supermarket building (7km; starting point for Walk 23), just inside **Gouvia** (🏨🏠✕🅿△). Those interested in Corfu's history may like to see the remains of the Venetian naval

arsenal near the marina. At the TSAVROS JUNCTION (9.5km 🏨🏠✕🅿) turn right; soon the floating chapel of Papandis★, shown on page 37, is seen. Bypassing the resort of **Dasia** (12.5km 🏨🏠△✕🅿), you soon reach the largest of the holiday villages, **Pyrgi/Ipsos** (15km 🏨🏠△✕🅿); it stretches out for a kilometre, beside a narrow pebble beach. Alternative walk 11-2 can end at Pyrgi, the northern end of the resort.*

---

*Just outside Pyrgi a road strikes left (off the first sharp bend) to Ag Markos (♗✕), a detour of 4km return. Icon and fresco enthusiasts will find two churches of interest here: Pantokrator, which boasts the best-preserved frescoes on the island (enquire at the local *cafeneion* to visit), and the nearby Byzantine chapel of Ag Merkourios★ (visit by prior arrangement with the Archaeological Museum in Corfu Town.

14

Venetian naval arsenal at Gouvia

Continuing towards Nissaki, there are exceptionally good views back over Corfu Town. The road descends to **Barbati** (19.5km ▲▲▲✕), and you catch a quick glimpse of its pretty pebbly beach, set at the foot of olive groves. **Nissaki** (23km ▲▲▲✕🖼) is the starting point for Walks 4-6 and 8; it's a good base for exploring the mountains and coast. Two superb picnic spots are in the neighbourhood: Katavolos (Short walk 4, photograph page 53) and at the start of Walk 5, near the Nissaki Beach Hotel (photograph page 57).

Winding in and out of the folds in the mountainside, the obvious signs of tourism begin to dwindle, and small, handsome white villages speckle the ridge-tops. Pull over at the KOULOURA/ KALAMI JUNCTION (30km 📷) and survey the scene — perhaps with a picnic in mind? Below is Kalami (▲✕), still exuding some of the charm so clearly conveyed in Lawrence Durrell's book, *Prospero's Cell*. Kouloura (✕), on the northern side of the point, also deserves its picture-postcard

rating. A few palms are dotted amongst the cypresses, olives and eucalyptus trees around the shoreline. A small jetty with just a scattering of fishing boats enhances the setting, which is better appreciated from a view-point (📷) 500m further along the road. Across the channel lies Albania, crowned with majestic peaks.

Climbing again, the countryside opens out. Another enticing cove, splendidly naked of buildings, reveals itself far below the road. A collar of turquoise sea edges the shoreline. If you haven't been down to the sea yet, a detour (7km return) to Ag Stefanos (▲▲▲✕) may be just what you're waiting for. The signposted turn-off lies 3km beyond the Kouloura/Kalami junction at **Sinies**, where Walk 5 ends. Keep left immediately after you turn off. Admittedly, tourism has already nibbled into this pretty sheltered cove, but it still retains some rustic charm. Alternative walk 5 sets out from here to explore the **Erimitis Nature Reserve** — a good place to stretch your legs.

15

The main tour continues towards Kassiopi. You begin to marvel at the wealth of trees in the landscape. In spring the floral splendour of the Judas tree, with its pink and purple clusters of flowers hanging from leafless branches, steals the show. **Kassiopi** (37km ✝🏨🏔🛏🍴🅿️△) is my favourite amongst the resorts. With its fishing-village flavour, it verges on recommendable. The remains of an Angevin fortress crown the scrub-covered headland behind the village. Many of the original walls and towers still stand impressively intact after some seven centuries. And it's worth stretching your legs by following a quiet road around the headland, visiting dazzling limestone ledges and tiny shingle coves. In autumn the ground is sprinkled with cyclamen, daisies and dandelions. Needless to say, there's excellent bathing here — head left on foot when you reach the port. In the Middle Ages, Kassiopi's church was the island's most venerated place of worship; it stands on the site of the Temple of Jupiter. Just around the corner from Kassiopi is the pretty seaside village of **Imerolia** (38km 🛏🍴). Walk 2 begins and ends here, surveying the scene shown opposite.

Your next turn-off comes up some 5km beyond Imerolia. Following signposting for Loutses and Ano Perithia, turn left into **Ag Ilias** (🛏🍴🅿️). In the village, keep left and uphill. Looping up through terraced hillsides, you briefly pass through olive groves. The islands of Othoni (the largest) and Erikoussa (the closest) come into sight, followed by the Antiniotissa Lagoon, nestled in a bed of

reeds on a tongue of flat land below. The mountains of Albania, a long line of peaks — which may be snow-capped until June —, trail off into the horizon. On reaching **Loutses** (🛏🍴), the landscape becomes noticeably rockier. The village trickles down a ridge. Oaks and turpentine trees begin appearing. Beyond Loutses, the untamed countryside shown on pages 60-61 envelops you: craggy, grassy slopes are littered with oaks, wild pears and holly oaks. **Ano Perithia** (51.5km 🍴) hides deep in the folds of Mt Pantokrator. Nestling within the surrounding hills, this once-deserted village is one of the prettiest spots on the island — ideal for picnicking. It was abandoned in the 1960s. But as recently as 70 years ago, it boasted a population of 3000, and *six* churches! Nowadays it boasts six *tavernas!* Wealthy people are buying and restoring some of the old properties in traditional style, and the village has been declared a Heritage Site by the Greek government. Walks 6-9 pass through here.

Back down on the main north coast road, some 300m further on turn off right to the **Antiniotissa Lagoon** and **Ag Spiridon** (61km 🏔🛏🍴), an intimate cove with a shallow limpid sea, where I highly recommend you stretch your legs on Walk 1.

Continuing west, you head along a sea-flat, where almond groves compete with the olives. The short stretch of pastureland is quickly interrupted by signs of development. Gorgeous Walk 3 begins at the 'roundabout' in **Acharavi** (67km 🏔🛏🍴🅿️). Just 200m past the roundabout, turn left towards Ag Pandelimon.

Ignore the road off left 700m uphill. Cutting inland, you climb into the interior, hugging ridges and skirting valleys, always in the shadow of Pantokrator. Garden plots spill out across the floors of valleys. Dark blades of cypress trees cut through the olive-green countryside. The drawn-out village of **Ag Pandelimon** (69.5km), visited in Walk 3, passes almost unnoticed — perhaps because the church is below the main road and not seen. At the junction just outside the village, continue straight ahead. Episkepsis appears, strung out on the ridge opposite. Entering **Episkepsis** (71.5km ✖), keep to the middle (widest) of the three roads ahead. Walk 8a visits this charming village, full

Kassiopi, from the hillside below Bodholakos (Walk 2)

Yes they are charming — but if you've never seen them before, be warned: these roadside shrines are testament to a fatal road accident at the spot where they are placed.

of colourful corners, one of them shown on page 2. A noticeable Venetian manor sits on the left in the village centre.

The route continues via **Sgourades** (76km), where comfortable old homes lean up against each other. Goats and sheep may cross the road. Under 1km outside Sgourades, fork left for Pantokrator (signposted for Petalia and Lafki). The ascent proper begins, and there are fine views across the northwest of the island. Twisting deeper into the bulwark of rock, you come upon a basin of vineyards and garden plots. Rounding a corner, **Strinilas** (82km ✕) appears, set in hillside boulders and foliage. An enormous elm shades the square. The local wine here is medium-sweet and considered by many Corfiots to be the best on the island. Ask for a *'dopio'*, if you want to try it. Strinilas is also visited in Walk 8a.

Beyond Strinilas, you cross a ridge and lonely Petalia comes into view, set back in a bare stepped basin. Just over the ridge before Petalia, turn right uphill, following signposting for Pantokrator. Less than 1km uphill, pull over for a fine view over Petalia and the northern escarpment (▣). Mounting the plateau, you curl around rocky, scrub-covered hillocks. The landscape becomes more stark. In spring the stones and rocks are covered in flowers; just a short stroll away from the car you can find asphodels, saxifrage, marigolds, irises, fritillaries,

veronicas, borage, and several varieties of wild orchids, tiny and ornate, often with the most amazing markings. Please don't pick the flowers! The panorama from the summit of **Mt Pantokrator** (88.5km ♦▣) is unsurpassed on the island. On really clear days, the toe of Italy in the north and the islands of Paxos and Antipaxos in the south can be seen — but during the hazy summer months only the whole of Corfu and the spellbinding sight of nearby Albania can be guaranteed! Ano Perithia stands out like a garden in this bleak landscape.

When you are saturated with views and you've visited the chapel shown on page 72, return to the SGOURADES/SPARTILAS JUNCTION below Strinilas (100km), where you first turned off for Pantokrator, and turn left. Heading south, you're confronted with a splendid coastal view, taking in the bays of Ipsos, Dafnila, Gouvia, and finally Potamos Bay, stretching all the way to Corfu Town. In autumn the surrounding hillsides are soaked in pink heather. Walk 9 begins at **Spartilas** (101.5km ▲✕▣), and alternative versions of Walk 11 can end there. This village is magnificently sited on the upper inclines of Pantokrator. Nowhere else on Corfu commands such a view. From here you drop down to the Nissaki road via an almost endless series of S-bends. Turn right (108.5km ☁), back to **Corfu Town** (124km).

Car tour 2: QUIET CORNERS OF THE NORTHWEST

**Corfu • Troumpeta • Valanio • Nimfes • (Roda) • Sidari •
(Peroulades • Magoulades) • Ag Stefanos • Arilas • Afionas •
Arkadades • Ag Georgios • Troumpeta • Corfu**

*108km/67mi; about 6 hours; Exit A
from Corfu Town (plan pages 8-9)*
Walks en route: 10, 11, 12, 14c,
15, 19, 20, 23; 13 is nearby

Picnic suggestions: All the
walks listed above feature picnic
spots shown by the symbol *P* on
the relevant walking maps.

O nce over the escarpment wall, you trail along ridges
and dip in and out of lush valleys. An array of villages
little changed over the centuries lies scattered across the
countryside. The beautiful bays along the west coast
provide good swimming spots — especially Ag Georgios
Bay, one of the most scenic on Corfu. If your return
coincides with sunset, drive up the hairpins of the Sokraki
road from Troumpeta Pass, to catch the island in one of its
mellower moods: from the escarpment wall, where no one
colour dominates the landscape, the countryside takes on
all the hues of the dying sun.

Follow Car tour 1 to the TSAVROS
JUNCTION (9.5km 🏔🏔🛆✕🍴),
then head left towards Paleokastritsa, passing through **Sgombou**
(🛆✕; Walks 19 and 20).
Leaving a pretty valley of cypress
trees, turn right for Sidari and
Roda (14km; signposted).
Climbing through trees (17.5km
🍴), come into **Skripero**
(18.5km). Notice the stately
villas on the left, some with
arcades. At **Troumpeta Pass**
(23km ✕📷), where Alternative
walks 11-1 and 11-2 begin, your
views sweep out over the central
lowlands of the north. And
behind you, the Ropa Plain, the
vast lake of pastureland shown
on pages 96-97, comes out of
hiding.
Descending into the north, the
hills and valleys become more
accentuated. Offshore lie the
sharp-edged Theapondinisi
Islands. Take the first turning

right beyond the pass (making
for Roda); then, 1.5km along,
turn sharp right again (signed for
Roda and Acharavi). This
narrow country road twists down
into a luxuriant valley full of trees
and gardens. Not far beyond an
abandoned, enclosed hermitage,
you enter **Valanio** (29km).
Squeezing through this rustic
village, keep right before

*Moni Pantokrator of Nimfes — a
pleasant picnic spot on Walk 10*

reaching the church, towards 'RODA' (indicated by a tiny sign on a wall ahead to the right). The road curls downhill into a wide, open valley, and crosses another stream.

At the first junction you come to, bear right *(not signposted)*. This road takes you uphill through **Kiprianades** (31.5km ♟). An eye-catching church, with a verandah, sits on the left a minute past this hamlet. A left turn at the next junction quickly brings you back down to the main road, where you keep right towards Roda. Half a kilometre along, not far past a restaurant, fork right to **Nimfes** (36km ✗; Walk 10), where you could drive (or walk in 15-20 minutes) to the old monastery shown on page 19 by taking the road at the left of the square or drive past the football ground to the waterfall by taking the road to the right of the square.

Continuing to the main Roda road, head right. But unless you want a closer look at this unim-

View over Armenades en route to Kavadades (not on the touring route)

has long since taken its toll on this beauty spot.

Return to the main road and drive westwards towards Avliotes.

Detours: From the PEROULADES JUNCTION (✸) you could make a 5km return detour (not in the main tour) to the impressive beach shown overleaf and on the cover. To reach it, head through Peroulades (▲✸) and follow signs 'To the Beach'. Logas (or 'Sunset') Beach (▲✸) is a narrow ribbon of sand at the foot of towering white bluffs. On your return through Peroulades, why not stretch your legs with a 15-20 minute walk to the viewpoint shown in the photograph on page 1? It's also possible to drive there; otherwise, park below the village square (leave plenty of room for the bus to turn round) and then use the notes on page 78 to start Walk 12 on Cape Drastis.

The main tour continues straight on to **Avliotes** (58km ▲✸), an unremarkable farming settlement, approached via a low valley embroidered in green squares. Judas trees line the side of the road. At the end of Avliotes, fork left for Ag Stefanos. Haphazard development has scarred the countryside's beautiful rolling green hills around here. The pleasant sandy beach at **Ag Stefanos** (62.5km ▲▲▲✸), with its backdrop of cliffs, is best seen from the chapel. To reach the beach and its restaurants, turn right at the junction.

For Arilas, the next stop, keep left. A gentle ascent takes you uphill to a T-junction, where you turn left. At the ARILAS

pressive resort (▲▲▲△✸➾⊕), turn left at the RODA JUNCTION (42km). The road bypasses Karoussades (46km ▲✸➾⊕), the largest village in the north. At a junction just over 4km further on (➾) turn right to **Sidari** (51km ▲▲▲✸➾), a sprawling resort on a long, but unremarkable sandy beach. Caiques sail to the Theapondinisi Islands from the jetty here (it's often a rough trip!). Half a kilometre along the shoreline, take the first turning right *(not signposted)*. At a T-junction just over the tidal stream, keep right, and park at the side of the road at the **Canal d'Amour★** (▲▲▲✸). This beautifully-eroded clay and marl shoreline, etched with coves, is a superb swimming spot — a good place to take a break on Walk 12a. The bare layered walls, fringed with heather and broom, stand out sharply against the turquoise sea. Local tradition has it that any girl who swims through the channel here — a short stretch of sea passage — while it's in shade, will win the man of her dreams. But tourism

right, signed for Ag Georgios Beach). The road is steep and winding. **Afionas Beach** (71.5km ♠✖) occupies the northern corner of the bay, which shows few signs of development. Continuing along the road, midway along the bay you climb above a cluster of beach-front houses. On reaching the crest of a hill, turn down to the right. The road briefly swings inland to skirt a swamp, before reaching the nucleus of **Ag Georgios** (73.5km ♠♠♠✖). Walks 14c and 15 visit the bay. About 1km along the beachfront, the way veers sharply back to the left and you head inland through a landscape of low-slung hills and valleys. Cypress trees make their mark on the countryside.

Keep right at the junction, where a road goes left to Dafni. Rising into the pretty hillside village of **Pagi** (78km), keep up to the right and, at the T-junction that follows immediately, turn left to drive through the village. Further on, another road joins from the right; continue along to the left, winding through olive-clad hills.

At the junction midway through **Arkadades** (83km), turn sharp right. Some 1.5km further on, just past **Kastellani** (🚌), you rejoin the SIDARI/CORFU ROAD. Ascend to the right here, to **Troumpeta Pass**, where Alternative walks 11-1 and 11-2 begin. now you return along the good road of your outward route (🚌). Go left at the PALEO-KASTRITSA JUNCTION, then keep straight ahead at the TSAVROS JUNCTION (98.5km 🚌), returning to **Corfu Town** in 108km.

JUNCTION (64.5km ♠✖🚌) head right for the beach at **Arilas** (♠♠♠✖). Gravia Island, a sharp oblong rock, sits not far offshore. The Cape Arilla promontory, shown on page 83, rises boldly out of the sea to the left. Continuing on, briefly follow the seashore. A kilometre along (having ignored the first right turn), fork right on a narrow road signposted for Afionas. The bumpy road winds its way up to T-junction, where you turn right to enchanting **Afionas** (69.5km ♠✖🖼). Keep in mind when parking that the bus turns round in the village square, so park *at least* 100m below the square, off the side of the road. Don't miss the unsurpassed views from the top of the ridge behind this village; see Walk 14b on page 83. You might also like to take a short walk to overlook Port Timone (Walk 14a).

Heading back out of Afionas, take the first right turn (a *sharp*

Car tour 3: CENTRAL CORFU'S VARIED LANDSCAPES

Corfu • Paleokastritsa • Lakones • Angelokastro • Makrades •
Troumpeta • Ropa Plain • Mirtiotissa Beach • (Glyfada Beach) •
Pelekas • Sinarades • Ag Gordis Beach • Kato Garouna • (Ano
Garouna) • Achilleion Palace • Corfu

*114km/71mi; about 6 hours; Exit
A from Corfu Town (plan pages
8-9). Roads are generally good, but
narrow and winding. The road to
Lakones is a series of hairpin bends
and might prove unnerving for
inexperienced drivers.*
Walks en route: 11-13, 15-23
Picnic suggestions: All the
walks listed above feature picnic

spots shown by the symbol *P* on
the relevant walking maps.
Opening hours
Paleokastritsa Monastery:
07.00-13.00, 15.00-20.00
(1.4-31.10); dress conserva-
tively: people wearing bathing
suits will not be admitted
Achilleion Palace: 09:00-16.00
daily

This is a tour that you can do at a leisurely pace, taking
time out for some leg-stretching short walks, perhaps
to some of the suggested picnic spots and then just a bit
further... If you are more fond of walking than driving,
break the tour into a two-day circuit and spice it up with
the many possible short walks. You could climb the flanks
of Mt Arakli (Shorter walk 16-1), to one of the finest views
in Europe, or check out the breathtaking perch of Angelokastro and the scant remains of its Byzantine fortress
(Shorter walk 16-3); stroll across the shepherds' pastures
by Gavrolimni Pond (Walks 19 and 20); scale the scrubby
peak of Ag Deka to the hidden Pantokrator monastery
(Walk 24); wander down to the beach Lawrence Durrell
thought the most beautiful in the world — Mirtiotissa
(Walk 22). All these exhilarating and seldom-visited spots
are accessible to everyone; for the most part, they are only
a short distance on foot.

Follow Car tour 2 for 14km,
where Car tour 2 turns right
towards Sidari. Here continue
straight ahead to **Paleokastritsa**★
(25km ♦♠♠△✕⊕☞), a top
priority on every tourist's agenda.
It's *the* resort on Corfu, and with
this comes all the benefits and
disadvantages of such a centre.
At the foot of the Arakli Hills, on
the edge of tumbling olive
groves, rest six enticing turquoise
coves, scooped out of the rocky
shoreline. Tourism may have
taken its toll, but no one can
deny that the setting, shown on

pages 12-13, is stupendous.
Walks 15-19 set out from
here.
Following the road straight
through the village, you come to
the sheer-sided wooded
promontory crowned by the
monastery. (There are traffic
lights at the foot of the
monastery drive, which may
involve a four-minute wait.) The
blindingly-white building dates
from the 18th and 19th
centuries; however, the monastery was founded in 1228. A
pleasant cloister garden lies

23

Achilleion Palace: its terraced garden affords panoramic views

inside the gates. You may find the collection of 17th- and 18th-century icons in the one-room museum of interest. The monks here don't hide their weariness of tourists. Entrance is free, but one is expected to put something into the offerings box — they may even remind you to do so, should you forget.

Leaving the monastery, you have an excellent view of Lakones (your next stop), strung out along a shelf in the escarpment wall over to the left. Retracing the route for some 3.5km, take the first road off left, signposted to Lakones. The steep climb up a series of S-bends affords superb views all the way. Olive trees arch over the road like large umbrellas; dark pockets of cypresses lie amidst them. Neat rock walls terrace the inclines. Approaching **Lakones** (33km ▲✕; Shorter walk 16-2) — where a traffic light operates a one-way system, perhaps involving a five-minute wait — the coves below unravel, and soon the view encompasses Lia-pades and the coastal hills. One

kilometre beyond the village, a balcony viewpoint (📷; with limited parking) provides the best spot to take in this magnificent panorama. From here the scars of tourism become minor flaws.

From the viewpoint take the first turn-off left, signposted to **Krini** (36km ▲✕). Remain on this road until it ends at the foot of **Angelokastro**★ (37km ▮📷; Shorter walk 16-3). Little remains of the castle, but the 325m/1000ft drops down to the sea from its perch are quite impressive! This Byzantine fortress is thought to have been built around the 12th century by Michael Angelos I. Corfu Town can be seen from the top; hence it was a good place from which to signal the approach of enemy vessels.

Return to the junction (lined with tourist stalls) just outside Krini. Turn immediately left (signposted to Makrades) and after 30m park outside an old school. Walk straight ahead for one minute, then fork left on a concrete lane which soon becomes a stony track. Follow the track for about 15 minutes (or, if you're in a 4WD vehicle, just continue straight on to the end of the track; see the map on page 85 at waypoint 5). I think this view () — over the bay of Ag Georgios — is every bit as fine as the outlook from the viewpoint past Lakones. Returning to the junction lined with tourist stalls, turn left. Continue uphill, past the edge of **Makrades** (⬧✖), to **Vistonas**

(40.5km ✖). Then slowly mount the escarpment, snatching a view back down over Krini, Makrades and Angelokastro. Pink heather (in autumn) and yellow broom (in spring) bring life to these harsh hillsides in their respective seasons. From the crest a panorama unfolds overlooking both the north and the south of the island. Pull over anywhere along here and take it all in. Remain along the crest of the escarpment all the way to

Angelokastro

Café in Krini; alley in Sinarades; Krini's lovely threshing floor

Troumpeta Pass (48km ✕🎞; Alternative walks 11-1, 11-2), then head right. Descending from the junction, you look out over central Corfu, rippled with wooded hills. Doukades, the next port of call, is the village snuggled up against the escarpment wall on the right. Some 3.5km down from Troumpeta, turn off right to **Doukades** (54.5km ⬣✕; Walk 21). This closely-knit hillside village has some fine houses in its midst. Leaving the village, ignore a road to the right and another to the left; keep straight downhill. On reaching the Paleokastritsa road (🏪), fork left. Some 800m along, on a bend, turn off *sharp* right towards Liapades. At the junction just below Liapades (⬣✕🏪; Walks 17-19), turn left, coming onto the edge of the **Ropa Plain** (Walks 19 and 20). Heading along through farm plots and vineyards, you're soon passing unfenced pastureland squared off by ditches. Some 5.2km along the Ropa Valley road, you pass the turn-off left for Gavrolimni Pond (a nice picnic spot) and Ag Noufures

(the chapel shown on page 98), signalled by a sign with a grass-hopper on it.

At the GIANADES/MARMARO JUNCTION, 1.2km further on, swing right and cut across the plain. After 2.5km head left at a three-way junction. At the next junction, 2.5km further on, turn left, and after 800m turn right over a bridge next to the entrance to the Corfu Golf Club (⛳). This brings you to the outskirts of Vatos. Soon after passing a petrol station (🏪), a right turn uphill leads to Vatos (⬣△✕), should you wish to see it. Otherwise, fork right 200m past the petrol station for Pelekas and Glyfada. The dark, wooded slopes of Ag Georgios loom above. This area is the setting for Walk 23, which crosses the island from west to east.

Although no longer as unspoilt as in the photograph on pages 102-103, **Mirtiotissa Beach** (⚓✕; Walk 22) is worth seeing. The turn-off is signposted about 1.3km along the Glyfada road. The track down to the beach is steep and rutted; it may be preferable to park partway down (perhaps at the taverna, if you want a meal) and walk. Five minutes past the beach the secluded Moni Mirtiotissa (Our Lady of the Myrtles) nestles amidst olive groves and pines. It is currently occupied by one monk who is deputed from Paleokastritsa; if he is there, it should be possible to gain access to the fenced and gated monastery, to visit the church — *if* you observe the appropriate dress code!

From Mirtiotissa, the tour returns 1km to the main road, where you turn right. Then, 1km further on, turn left at the next GLYFADA/PELEKAS JUNCTION (unless you want to see Glyfada Beach.) A steady climb through olive groves brings you into **Pelekas** (76.5km ♗⏰▲✕). Turn *sharp left* just past the first church reached on entering the village. This goes to a viewpoint called the '**Kaiser's Throne**' (▲✕▣). In late autumn, the profusion of crocuses covering this peak may momentarily distract you from the wonderful panorama. You look across to Corfu Town and Pantokrator, down into the Ropa Valley and over towards the small mountains of Garouna and Ag Deka.

Returning to **Pelekas**, continue through the village and rounding a hairpin bend to the left. Then turn right at the first junction. Travelling along a valley floor patched in vineyards, after 3.5km come to a second junction, where you bear right into colourful **Sinarades** (83.5km ⏰▲✕). This charming village still retains its country character. At the T-junction (☎) outside Sinarades, head right to **Ag Gordis**

(87.5km ⏰▲✕). Its scenic location has made this village a very popular spot. To avoid the centre near the beach (parking is virtually impossible), descend past the hillside apartments then, *just as the road flattens out,* turn left for Kato Garouna, winding high up the olive-clad inclines of Mt Garouna.

Everyone bypasses **Kato Garouna** (89.5km ✕), which looks unappealing on approach. But this cheerful little hamlet is bursting with colour and character. Turning left at the (unsigned) junction in the village, swing back towards Corfu Town, circling the valley. Keep left all the way, ignoring turn-offs to Ano Pavliana and Ag Mattheos. The valley walls become steeper, with terracing chiselled out of the hillsides. At **Ag Theodori** (93.5km ✕), you come to the turn-off right for Ano Garouna (✕▣; Walk 24a) — a detour of 3.5km return. Ano Garouna also boasts a lovely view over the valley and a corner of Ag Gordis.

The main tour passes this turn-off. Continue straight ahead 5km to the SINARADES/CORFU ROAD and keep right. At the GASTOURI JUNCTION, 3km along, turn right uphill and pass through **Gastouri** (⏰▲✕). After 2km you reach **Achilleion Palace★** (▮M▣), a whim of the Empress of Austria. This ostentatious palace (1892) was a retreat from the goings-on of the Hapsburg Court. After her assassination, it remained vacant until Kaiser Wilhelm II bought it, adding a few touches of his own.

Keep on this road to the coast, then head left on the main road, back to **Corfu Town** (114km).

Car tour 4: NOOKS AND CRANNIES IN THE SOUTH

Corfu • (Messongi) • Hlomos • Issos Beach • Argirades • Kouspades •
Perivoli • Lefkimmi • Kavos • Gardiki Castle • Korission Lagoon •
Ag Mattheos • Corfu

*144km/90mi; about 7 hours; Exit B
from Corfu Town (plan pages 8-9).
The main south road is well-surfaced
but busy; the tour also follows some
narrow winding roads.*

Walks en route: 24-30
Picnic suggestions: All the
walks listed above feature picnic
spots shown by the symbol *P* on
the relevant walking maps.

The highlight of this tour is 'Lake' Korission — really a
lagoon. It's a unique, untouched spot, offering something for everyone. Birds — of both varieties — for the
bird-watchers, flowers (orchids and catchfly) for the
botanists, a shallow beach for the sun-seekers … and, best
of all, peace and quiet for everyone. Beyond Argirades there
is little of interest for the passing tourist, but for the walkers
among you I've included characterless Kavos, where Walk
29a is highly recommended, and the starkly beautiful salt
pans on Cape Lefkimmi (Walk 30, shown below).

Leave Corfu Town from San
Rocco Square/Platia Georgiou
Theotoki and Dimoulitsa Street,
following signs for the airport/
Lefkimmi (Exit B). At the
LEFKIMMI JUNCTION (5km), turn
left. (This tour heads south via
the coastal road. If you're already
familiar with this route, you may
like to try the alternative inland
route described in the panel
opposite.)
Heading into Perama, you get a
glimpse (☉) of the Vlakerena
Convent, joined to the shore by a
causeway, and Pondikonisi
(Mouse Island). This wonderful
setting, shown on page 37,
represents Corfu on every
brochure. But from **Perama**
(7km ⌂▲✕△⌂) to Benitses the
coastline is built-up and unattrac-
tive. Colour in the gardens and

the profusion of trees do, however, soften the blow. Past
Perama, you're just above the
blue-green sea. Soon you pass
the **Kaiser's Bridge★** (✕), a
fancy marble jetty once joined to
the **Achilleion Gardens★** (Car
tour 3) by a bridge, of which a
segment remains.
Benitses (12km ⌂▲✕⊕),
where Walk 24a ends and Walks
25a-c begin, rests at the foot of a
thickly-wooded hillside. The
luxuriant wild garden shown on
page 110 lies deep in a valley, a
mere 20 minutes' walk from
here. If you're a walker, try some
version of Walk 25; if you're not
a walker, but you don't mind a
few steep steps, head up to the
waterworks garden: follow the
start of Walk 25 on page 111,
then use the map on page 113 to

continue up the valley after climbing steps through an 'arch' of greenery.

Back on the main road, the remains of a 3rd-century Roman villa suggest that Benitses has been a seaside resort for many centuries (there is also a Roman bathhouse in the village).

Beyond Benitses, development thins out to an odd hotel here and there. There is a lovely view of the coastline hills trailing off towards the tail of the island just before **Moraitika** (19.5km ▲▲▲✕➾⊕).

Approaching the MESSONGI JUNCTION (20.5km), you pass through another eyesore of touristic development. Turn right at the junction, heading inland. At the T-junction at **Ano Messongi** (▲✕➾) turn left, following the main road over a concrete bridge. *(This is where the alternative inland route joins from the right.)* Just over the Messongi Bridge, the road to Ag Mattheos turns off right. Ignore it and keep straight on, leaving the tourist belt behind. The road is wider and faster going, as you travel through olive groves, with the occasional vineyard and garden in their midst. From now on the tour turns off this main road at regular intervals.

The first two side-trips branch off opposite each other at **Linia** (27.5km ✕➾). First turn off left for Hlomos (signposted); on your return you will make for Issos Beach from the turn-off just opposite. The ascent to Hlomos

Alternative inland route

Keep straight on at the LEFKIMMI JUNCTION. Curve right towads Paleokastritsa after 2.5km,and 1km further on turn left for Ag Deka (signposted). Snake up the steep slopes of Mt Ag Deka, covered with loose scatterings of cypress trees. The centre of the island quickly unravels as you climb. Corfu Town and the Khalikiopoulos Lagoon lie not far below. Three kilometres uphill, you pass **Ag Deka** (Walk 24), a cluster of houses stepping the hillside, with a superb outlook over the gulf to Pantokrator and Albania. Further around the now-sheer inclines, Benitses comes into sight below, cushioned between hills, at the water's edge. Epirus, over the channel, is a series of rounded ridges. A visit to **Halidata, Dafnata** and **Komianata**, charming pristine villages with very old homes, is recommended. They are visited on Walk 25. The turn-off is the first left beyond Ag Deka. Back on the main road, turn left, to cross over the ridge and descend into the Messongi Valley, woven in olive groves and garden plots. Down on the plain, you pass through the small farming settlement of **Strongili** (Walk 25c), then rejoin the main touring route at **Ano Messongi**.

The salt pans of Lefkimmi (Walk 30)

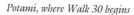

Potami, where Walk 30 begins

Walk 28 visits this clean, wild stretch of seashore, which sweeps away to the right. For those who like some sand in their sarnies, it's a great place to picnic. The dark slopes of Ag Mattheos rise in the background (photograph page 118). You can climb the crusty sand formations rising from the dunes, five minutes' walk away, for uninterrupted views of Lake Korission.

The next turning off the main road is at **Argirades** (41.5km ⬤✕✉). Halfway through the village, at a bright yellow kiosk with an awning, turn left *(not signposted)*. Dropping down through olive groves, you cross an intensively-cultivated basin. An abundance of trees — walnut, loquat, Judas, fig — grows amidst the olives. At the PETRETI/NOTOS T-JUNCTION, 2.5km downhill, head left to **Kouspades** (45km ⬤✕). This *is* a whitewashed picture-postcard village. It's bright and spotless, with very old homes in its midst. You can park off the junction, where you enter the village, and wander up to the left.

Detours: From Kouspades there are three possible detours to visit pleasant villages or picnic spots (not included in the overall kilometre readings). Using the map on pages 116-117, you could visit Korakades, some 1.5km along to the right — a sleepy little settlement facing abandon. The picnic setting highlighted here is a tranquil spot amongst the deserted houses, in the quiet of olive groves. Or there's Boukari (⬤✕), a pretty seaside village on a quiet stretch of coastline 1km north of Kouspades. Petreti

affords good views over the Korission Lagoon and, 1.5km uphill, a roadside viewpoint (📷) makes an ideal spot from which to enjoy the view. Entering **Hlomos** (31.5km ✕📷), park in the small parking bay just past the colourful Sirtaki Taverna (be sure to leave room for the bus to turn round). For superb views walk a further 100m into the village and follow the signs up to the church shown on page 115, which sits on the hillside above the village. A fine panorama awaits you, encompassing the washed-out hills of Epirus, Lefkimmi Bay, and Cape Lefkimmi tapering off into a fine line. Even Paxos seems close by. Hlomos, visited in Walk 26, is not your typical whitewashed picture-postcard village; it overflows with character. Houses straddle a steep hillside crowded with a maze of alleys. Every house takes advantage of the panoramic views.

Back at the main road, cross over and wind along through olive trees, vineyards and fields to the dunes of **Issos Beach** (37km).

(♠✕), a little further east, is a small and unspoiled fishing village with a narrow beach. A lovely picnic spot just south of the village is the pretty little cove of Notos, at the foot of an olive grove.

Getting acquainted with the southern tip of Corfu is best done on foot. The drive beyond Argirades is unexciting, and Kavos and Lefkimmi would be best avoided. But Walks 29a and 30 are highly recommended for everyone; they go to unfrequented corners. The touring route is straightforward: follow the main road through **Perivoli** (54.5km ♠✕♟), where Walks 26a and 28c end. Then turn off (58.5km) to **Lefkimmi** (61km ♠✕♟⊕), the largest village in the south. This neglected sprawl is really three adjacent villages (Ano Lefkimmi, Lefkimmi and Potami). Bird-watchers may like to visit the rather desolate but beautiful marshes and salt pans near Alikes, shown on pages 28-29, the setting for Walk 30. Otherwise, after crossing the picturesque Potamos Estuary (where Walk 30 starts; photograph opposite), continue straight on. (But a left turn immediately over the river would take you alongside the river to a quiet beach less than 2km away.)

Continue through **Kavos** (66km ♠♠✕⊕), until you reach a T-junction at the end of this resort. Turn right here, for 'Beach'. About 200m further on, turn right again (*not signposted*). (But if you want to try Walk 29a to the ruins of Moni Panagia, keep *left* here; then, after 100m turn right on a gravel track and park.)

Beyond **Spartera** (70km ✕▭) the tour meanders amongst the hills, passing through small rural settlements: **Dragotina, Neochori, Bastatika** (turn left in the village, signposted to Ag Gordis Beach and in Greek to Paleochori), **Paleochori** (✕; keep right at the junction in the centre), and **Kritika** (turn right in the village for Lefkimmi). You emerge on the CORFU TOWN ROAD at a junction (79km ♟) south of Lefkimmi.

Turning left here, return to **Ano Messongi** and, just past the petrol station (96.5km ♟), turn left towards Ag Mattheos. Some 2.5km along, turn left again to towards the 13th-century Byzantine fortress of Gardiki. At a junction barely 1km along, turn left. Soon an impressive wall and tower gate rise on a mound in front of you. All that remains of **Gardiki Castle** (▉) is the exterior octagonal wall with its eight towers. Walks 28b and c start here. Continue beyond the fortress, then take the first left turn (102km), to **Halikouna Beach** (♠✕) and **Lake Korission** (700m further on a rough dirt road).

Circling the end of this shallow lagoon, you come to the beach. A causeway of grassy dunes separates the lagoon from the sea. The chaste beauty of the lagoon and the surrounding countryside with its reeds, fields and solitary dwellings, is a world apart from the usual olive-clad hills of Corfu. Grey mullet is farmed in the lagoon for its roe, which is made into *taramasalata*. A very rewarding easy leg-stretcher might be to follow Walk 28 along the dunes to the picturesquely sited fish farm by

Walks 26a and 28c: haystacks outside Perivoli. Below: all versions of Walk 28 skirt the south side of Lake Korission, where you'll see a bridge over the canal and a fish farming hut (both have been updated since this photograph was taken).

the canal linking the lagoon to the sea, in the setting shown above.

Botanists can while away the hours here, seeking out the loose-flowered orchid, *Silene colorata* (catchfly), sea stock, sea rocket, sea holly and various sea blites, as well *Medicago marina* (sea medick) and *Otanthus maritimas*. Bird life abounds here in winter and spring, but dwindles in summer. In winter you can see mallards and teal, and many waders — shovellers, pintails, wigeon, and dotterels. Even more birds visit in spring: avocets, on rare occasions glossy ibis, long-legged stilts, small waders like the oyster-catcher, stone curlew, little egret, grey, purple and squacco herons ... as well as cormorants, gulls and terns — if you're lucky, a white-winged black tern.

From here return to Gardiki Castle and, just beyond it, bear left for Proussadi Beach, circling the foot of Mt Ag Mattheos. This

part of the drive is my favourite: the gentle inclines harbour a vast museum of olive trees, with magnificent specimens arching out over the road. Narrow dirt lanes forking off left go to pretty coves, including **Skidi** and **Proussadi** (⬥✕). Keep right where a road heads left to Paramona (▲▲⬥✕).

Squeezing through a passageway in the hills, you reach the outskirts of **Ag Mattheos** (114.5km ⬥✕), a sprawling hillside village. A road joins from the right. At the next junctions, keep following signs for Corfu Town (Kerkyra). But if you've plenty of time left, I suggest the toughish ascent of Mt Ag Mattheos (Walk 27); see page 118 to park. Descend through a landscape of mossy olive groves, spiced with thickets of cypress. A brief ascent follows, up a winding road to the hilltop village of **Vouniatades** (117km), overlooking the Messongi Valley. Dropping into this broad basin, you meander through groves patched with bright pink heather in autumn or sweet-scented myrtle in spring. Hills rise all around you, and villages peep out of the wooded ridges.

On reaching the Kato Garouna junction (120.5km), keep right and, at **Ag Theodori** (✕) pick up the notes for Car tour 3 from the 93.5km-point (page 27), to return to **Corfu Town** (144km).

● Walking

Few tourists realise the scope Corfu offers for walking, but this book has enough walks to keep insatiable ramblers occupied for a solid month. For beginners, Corfu is an ideal place to start: the scenic rewards and the countryside experiences soon become addictive. If you're not a walker, the friendly, quieter countryside will soon turn you into one.

The 'Landscapes' series is built around walks and excursions that can be made *in day trips* from your home base, even if you choose not to hire a car. So all the walks in this book were originally conceived as day excursions *accessible by bus* from Corfu Town. These days many people hire cars and prefer circular walks. We have tried to cater for motorists in this Eighth edition, but do bear in mind that many old donkey trails — especially those crossing the Pantokrator Massif in the north — were built to take villagers from one place to another: they are all linear. Circular walks are indicated by a ⊖ symbol in the Contents. Look for the 🚗 symbol under 'Access' at the head of the relevant walk (where we also give you waypoints so that you can set your satnav to get you to the starting point). But even if a walk is more suitable for bus users, there's no reason why you should not tackle it from your car. You can walk from A to B and take a bus back to your car — or, to be on the safe side, drive to the end of the walk, leave your car there, and take a bus to the starting point.

Consider combining walks. We've indicated where routes overlap on the walking maps. But, for safety's sake, only link up walks by following paths described in these notes or by using roads or tracks; don't try to cross rough country (which might be dangerous) or private land (where you might not have the right of way).

There are walks in this book for everyone.

Beginners: Start on the walks graded ● or ●, or look for the *P* symbols on the walking maps; these indicate picnic places that can be reached after a very short walk.

Experienced walkers: If you are accustomed to rough terrain and are feeling fit, you should be able to enjoy all these walks. Some require agility, and a couple will demand a head for heights as well. Take into account the season and weather conditions: don't attempt the more strenuous

33

The Corfu Trail

Corfu's own long-distance footpath was opened in 2002, after several years of planning and hard work. It follows a meandering route of 200km from the island's southernmost tip at Cape Asprokavos (visited on Walk 29) to its northern termination at Ag Spiridon (Walk 1). The approximate route of the whole trail is shown on the touring map; the walking maps show where it coincides with routes in this book.

The Trail avoids heavily developed areas, and in passing through the island's rural regions, takes in as many of its finest locations as possible — some well known, some obscure. It links beauty spots, beaches, picturesque mountain villages, deserted hamlets, viewpoints, monuments, monasteries and museums. It follows quiet country roads, lanes and forest tracks, but also many centuries-old cobbled mule-paths — *the kalderimia,* once used by local people getting from village to village.

The route is waymarked with yellow aluminium signs attached to permanent features and augmented with yellow paint arrows, dots and flashes (paint marks are most common in the mountainous areas).

Readers wishing to explore the Corfu Trail should obtain a copy of the excellent *Companion Guide to the Corfu Trail* by Hilary Whitton Papeiti (the route's creator), currently published only as a pdf download priced at €10; see the author's website for details: www.corfutrailguide. com. She has also written other walking guides for the island (available from the same website), but unfortunately no publication date is given for any of them, and we found some changes on the ground while researching this edition.

Over half the walks in this Sunflower guide share routes used by the Corfu Trail, so you will almost certainly come across Corfu Trail signing and waymarks from time to time. But *don't* just follow these waymarks blindly without reading the text, or you may easily end up on the wrong path and walk further than you need!

Olive groves are pleasant picnic spots. This photograph was taken 20 minutes below Episkepsis on Walk 8a.

walks in high summer; protect yourself from the sun and carry ample water. **Hardy hikers** should head for the Pantokrator Hills — they'll test your stamina!

Grading, waymarking, maps, GPS

We've tried to give you a quick overview of each walk's **grade** in the Contents (although we've not had space to list *all* the walks). Here is an explanation of the three gradings of walks in this guide:

● very easy — more or less level (perhaps with a short climb to a viewpoint); good surfaces underfoot; easily followed

● easy-moderate — ascents/descents of no more than about 300-500m/ 1000-1800ft; good surfaces underfoot; easily followed

● moderate-strenuous — ascents/descents may be over 500m/1800ft; variable surfaces underfoot — you must be sure-footed and agile; possible route-finding problems in poor visibility

Any of the above grades may be followed by:

❗ *possibility* of vertigo — for those with no head for heights at all

It's always encouraging to see **waymarking** along the route. But, unless we specifically advise you to follow it, don't *rely* on waymarking. Only rarely are walks in this book waymarked — except where they coincide with the Corfu Trail (see opposite). While you may see waymarks on some stretches of the walks, it is *important that you follow the notes in the book.*

The **maps** in this book are based on Openstreetmap mapping (see page 2), very heavily annotated from our notes and GPS work in the field. We hope that these maps, which *cover almost the whole island* and which we have found to be *very* accurate on the ground, will be a boon to walkers. It is a pity that we have to reproduce them at only 1:50,000 to keep the book to a manageable size; some walkers buy both the paperback *and* download a pdf file of the same book from our website to print out the maps at a larger size. If you want coverage of the whole island on one sheet, see the maps mentioned on page 6.

Free **GPS track** downloads and **height profiles** are available for all these walks: see the Corfu page on the Sunflower website. Please bear in mind, however, that GPS readings should *never* be relied upon as your sole reference point, as conditions can change overnight. *But even if you don't use GPS*, these maps are so accurate that you can easily compare them with Google Maps on your smartphone and pinpoint your exact position. And it's great fun dragging our GPX files over Google Earth to preview the walks in advance!

What to take

If you're already on Corfu when you find this book, and you haven't any special equipment such as a rucksack or walking shoes with ankle support, you can still do some of the walks — or you can buy some equipment at one of the sports shops in Corfu Town. For each walk in the book the *minimum* year-round equipment is listed. Where walking boots are required there is, unfortunately, no substitute: you will need to rely on the grip and ankle support they provide, as well as their waterproof qualities. You may find the following checklist useful:

walking boots (or stout shoes with thick non-slip soles)
waterproof rain gear (outside summer months)
long-sleeved shirt (sun protection)
bandages and band-aids
extra pair of (long) socks
windproof (zip opening)
sunglasses, sunhat, suncream
whistle, torch, gps/smartphone (the **emergency number is 112**)
up-to-date transport timetable
spare bootlaces
plastic bottle with plenty of drinking water
long trousers, tight at the ankles (sun and tick protection)
insect repellent, antiseptic cream
knives and openers
fleece
plastic groundsheet
small rucksack

Please bear in mind that I have not done *every* walk in this book under *all* weather conditions. For that reason, I have listed under 'Equipment' all the gear you might need, depending on the season. I rely on your good judgement to modify the list accordingly. Beware of the sun and the effects of dehydration. It's tempting to walk in shorts and to forget that, with the sun behind you, the backs of your legs (and the back of your neck) are getting badly burned. **Always** carry a long-sleeved shirt and long trousers to put on when you've had enough sun, and **always wear a sunhat**. Take your lunch in a shady spot and carry plenty of water and fruit.

Where to stay

If your holiday is going to be a walking one, the most convenient place to stay is Corfu Town. All the buses leave from there. Your next best choice, in terms of public transport *only,* is along the touristy east coast, anywhere between Benitses and Ipsos: Perama, Kanoni, Kontokali, Gouvia. Away from the tourists and the coast, Potamos is another good choice. Staying in Kassiopi, Nissaki, Paleo-kastritsa, Ag Gordis or Kavos will limit your walking to short walks, especially outside peak season when the bus services are limited.

Renting a car solves the problem of getting to and from areas poorly served by buses. Car hire does have its disadvantages, since many walks are linear. (But remember that a car can be used in combination with the buses, or you can arrange to be collected by a taxi or friends who will take you back to your car.) You could also invest in a moped — they're cheap and will open up the whole island for you, inexpensively! Outside peak season finding a room is no problem (just ask at the local taverna or *cafeneion*), and making overnight stops between walks is great fun.

Weather

The kindest months for walking on Corfu are on either side of summer: April to June and September to October. July and August (with temperatures in the 30's) are hot and sticky; the only walking you'll enjoy at this time is to and from the beach.

Spring is announced in April with warmth in the sun and an extravaganza of wild flowers, but the rain isn't over yet. By June a rainy day is considered unlucky, and in July and August, a phenomenon. Towards the end of

Pondikonisi (Mouse Island)

September there's a freshness in the air again, with an occasional passing thunderstorm. In October it's time for a fleece and, as the month progresses, the cloudy days turn to rainy days. It's not the time for a beach holiday, but the haze-free cerulean sky and lush green fields, with their lavish pockets of autumn flowers, make this an exhilarating time to walk.

In summer the prevailing wind is the *maestros,* a strong nor'westerly which offers slight relief from the relentless hot days and gives cool, more comfortable nights. This gusty wind can last for several days. Another, but less common wind, is the *pounentes* — an ineffectual westerly breeze. A wind that will bother you on rare occasions is the *sirocco* — a hot, sticky, uncomfortable southeasterly that blows for short periods between July and August. It's recognised by its hazy skies. Fortunately this weather is not seen every year.

The prevailing winter wind is the *ostria,* a damp, mild wind from the south. January and February are the coldest months, with temperatures dropping (especially when the *sirocco levante* — SE by E — sweeps in off the snow-clad Epirus Mountains, bringing stormy weather). Ideal winter walking weather is brought by the crisply-cool *levante,* which guarantees clear sunny days.

Outside summer — mid June to mid September — be prepared for all kinds of unpredictable weather! Happy hiking.

Things that bite or sting

In general **dogs** are not a problem. On walks where we have encountered troublesome dogs, we warn you in advance. Pastoral dogs kick up a fuss if you venture too near their flocks/herds, but few are ever more than threatening. If dogs worry you, consider investing in a 'Dog Dazer' — an ultrasonic device which persuades aggressive dogs to back off, without harming them. You can order one online; various suppliers sell them.

Snakes are a more important problem. Fortunately only a couple are dangerous — the horn viper and the montpellier. The horn viper, easily recognised by its nose-horn and the zigzag or lozenge pattern down its back, is dangerous because it does not move out of your way! All other snakes are as frightened of you as you are of them. The montpellier, a dark grey to black fellow, is much less dangerous. Its fangs are at the rear of its upper jaw and unless it is able to get a good grip on its victim — unlikely

*Goats and shady olive groves —
one of the most enduring images
of walking on Corfu.*

when being trodden on — it cannot inject the venom. The biggest snake you'll see is the harmless, phlegmatic four-lined snake, which can reach 250cm/8ft. May and June is when the snakes come out to play … and September/October to a lesser extent. When walking in long grass, *always wear long trousers, socks, and shoes or boots — **never sandals***. Take a long stick to beat the grass, and be vigilant around springs and water sources in high summer.

Scorpions are nocturnal creatures, and the only time you'll encounter them is when you move logs or rocks. Do so carefully. Their sting is not dangerous, just painful.

Bees and **wasps** abound in summer, particularly around water. Approach all water sources and ponds, etc with care. If you're allergic to stings, make sure you have the necessary medicine with you.

Perhaps the biggest nuisance (but only in summer) is the **horse-fly**. Keeping them off you is more exhausting than the walk itself. Long trousers and long-sleeved shirts lessen the problem.

Avoid **ticks** by wearing long socks.

You'll also encounter, or hear, lots of **hunters**. They blast away at anything that moves or flies. Don't be afraid to shout and let them know you're around!

The **drinking water** in village fountains is safe but, in outlying areas, **wells have been polluted** by fertilisers.

A country code for walkers and motorists

The experienced rambler is used to following a 'country code', but the tourist out for a lark may unwittingly cause damage, harm animals, and even endanger his own life. Do heed this advice:

- **Do not light fires.** Stub out all cigarettes.
- **Do not frighten animals.** The goats and sheep you may encounter on your walks are not tame. By making loud noises or trying to touch or photograph them, you may cause them to run in fear and be hurt.
- **Walk quietly** through all farms, hamlets and villages, leaving all gates just as you found them. Gates do have a

purpose, usually to keep animals in — or out of — an area.

■ **Protect all wild and cultivated plants.** Don't try to pick wild flowers or uproot saplings. Obviously fruit and crops are someone's private property and should not be touched.

■ **Never** walk over cultivated land.

■ **Take all your litter away with you.**

■ **Do not take risks.** Do not attempt walks beyond your capacity and *never* walk alone. Always tell a responsible person exactly where you are going and what time you plan to return. Remember, if you become lost or injure yourself, it may be a long time before you are found. On any but a very short walk near villages, it's a good idea to take along a torch and a whistle, as well as extra food and clothing. *Always take plenty of water!*

Greek for walkers

In the major tourist areas you hardly need to know any Greek at all, but once you are out in the countryside a few words of the language will be helpful. Here's one way to ask directions in Greek *and understand the answers you get!* First memorise the few 'key' and 'secondary' questions

View from Ag Deka (Walks 24 and 25b) across the airport — to Corfu Town and the mountains of Albania

given below. Then, always follow your key question with a **second question demanding a yes *(ne)* or no *(ochi)* answer**. (By the way, Greeks invariably raise their heads to say 'no', which looks to us like the beginning of a 'yes'! By the way, 'ochi' (no) might be pronounced as **o**-hee, **o**-shee or even **oi**-ee.)

Following are the two most likely situations in which you may have to use some Greek. The dots (...) show where you will fill in the name of your destination. Ask locally for help with pronunciation; accented syllables are shown in the Index beginning on page 135.

■ Asking the way
The key questions

English	Approximate Greek pronunciation
Hello, good day, greetings	**Hair**-i-tay
Please —	**Sas** pa-ra-ka-**loh** —
where is	**pou-ee**-nay
the road that goes to ...?	o **thro**-mo stoh ...?
the footpath that goes to ...?	ee mono-**pati** stoh ...?
the bus stop?	ee **stassis**?
Many thanks.	Eff-hah-ree-**stoh** po-li.

Secondary question leading to a yes/no answer

English	Approximate Greek pronunciation
Is it here?	**Ee**-nay eth-**o**?
Is it there?	**Ee**-nay eh-**kee**?
Is it straight ahead?	**Ee**-nay kat-eff-**thia**?
Is it behind?	**Ee**-nay **pee**-so?
Is it to the right?	**Ee**-nay thex-**ya**?
Is it to the left?	**Ee**-nay aris-teh-**rah**?
Is it above?	**Ee**-nay eh-**pa**-no?
Is it below?	**Ee**-nay **kah**-to?

■ Asking a taxi driver to take you somewhere and return for you, or asking a taxi driver to collect you somewhere

English	Approximate Greek pronunciation
Please —	**Sas** pa-ra-ka-**loh** —
would you take us to ... ?	tha **pah**-reh mas stoh ... ?
Come and pick us up	**El**-la na mas **pah**-reh-teh
at ... (place) at ... (time)	apo ... stees ...

(Instead of memorising the hours of the day, simply point out on your watch the time you wish to be collected.)

Since you may have to rely on taxis for some walks, you might ask your hotel to find a driver who speaks good English. (In the resorts, all taxi drivers speak at least some English.) I'd also recommend you take an inexpensive phrase book. An especially useful book is Tom Stone's *Essential Greek Handbook*, which you should be able to find on the web. It has many key phrases and pronunciation hints, plus a wealth of practical information.

Organisation of the walks

The 60 long and short walks in this book are grouped in four general areas: around Mt Pantokrator and the northeast, the northwest, the centre of the island, and the south. You might begin by considering the large fold-out touring map inside the back cover. Here you can see at a glance the overall terrain, the road network, and the orientation of the walking maps in the text. Quickly flipping through the book, you'll find that there's at least one photograph for each walk.

Having selected one or two potential excursions from the map and the photographs, look over the planning information at the beginning of each walk. Here you'll find walking times, grade, equipment, and how to get there/return. If the grade and equipment specifications are beyond your scope, don't despair! *There's almost always a short or alternative version of a walk* and, in most cases, these are less demanding of agility and equipment. If it still looks too strenuous for you, remember to look at the P symbols on the walking maps: these picnic suggestions allow you to savour a walk's special landscape with minimum effort.

The text of each walk begins with an introduction to the overall landscape and then describes the route in detail. The **large-scale maps** (all 1:50,000 and all with north at the top) have been drawn to show current routes and key waypoints. **Times** are given for reaching certain landmarks. To work out how your walking pace compares with ours, start out with a couple of the easier walks. This is particularly important if you are relying on public transport at the end of a hike. You'll soon see how your pace compares with ours. Since we always do our research out of season when it's cooler (and cheaper!), it would be a good idea when planning to **add up to 50% to our walking times**, to allow for dawdling ... *and the heat!*

Many of the **symbols** used on the walking maps are self-explanatory, but below is a key

▬▬ main road	🗺 Corfu Trail and surface underfoot	❶❷ start/end.waypoint
▬▬ secondary road		⚘↑ garden.turbine
▭ 4WD track	⛪ church, monastery. chapel	♁ ♁ pylon.aerial
▬ jeep track	⊞† cemetery.shrine	P picnic spot (see page 10)
------ footpath	⛏⚒ factory.quarry	👓 best views
route of main walk and direction	🚐🚗 bus stop.parking	📖 page reference: map continuation
alternative route	♪ spring, tank etc	
other walk	▪ castle, palace	☼⌒ watermill.cave

Walk 1: CAPE AGIA EKATERINIS

Circuit for motorists
Distance/time: 4.5km/2.8mi;
1h30min
Grade: ● easy, but the coastal
path is very rocky, and there is
little shade
Equipment: boots or stout shoes
with good ankle support, sunhat,
suncream, sunglasses, swimwear,
picnic, water
Picnic: behind Ag Spiridon
beach (shade), first cove (no
shade), ruined monastery (shade),
second lagoon (no shade)
Access: 🚌 to/from the beach/
church at Ag Spiridon (**O**;
39° 48.931'N, 19° 51.751'E)
Alternative walk for bus users
Distance/time: 6.3km/4mi; 2h

Grade/Equipment/Picnic as for
motorists
Access: 🚌 to the Ag Ilias/
Loutses junction (**a**); Loutses
bus; journey time 1h15min, or
Kassiopi to Sidari bus; journey
time 10min (Timetables 11, 13)
Notes: From the bus stop at the
Ag Ilias junction, walk
northeast downhill and take the
first turn-off to the right. Keep
straight downhill to the beach at
Ag Spiridon (**O**), then pick up
the circuit for motorists below.
Follow it to the 45min-point,
then use the map below to follow
the CORFU TRAIL 35 minutes,
to the **Portes junction** bus stop
(**b**), for a Kassiopi to Roda 🚌.

This short walk is suitable for everyone, from kids to grannies. If you find the rocky coastal path hard going, you can switch to the track a short way inland. Cape Ekaterinis, with its lagoon, tidal streams, and small coves, is very picturesque — and tranquil outside high season. Pines and cypress trees also make a pleasant change from the ubiquitous olive.

The walk starts from the CHURCH at **Ag Spiridon** (which is the northern termination of the 200km-long CORFU TRAIL): continue west behind the main beach. This headland is refreshingly unspoilt, and the shallow sandy beach is ideal for children. The **Antiniotissa Lagoon** lies behind the beach,

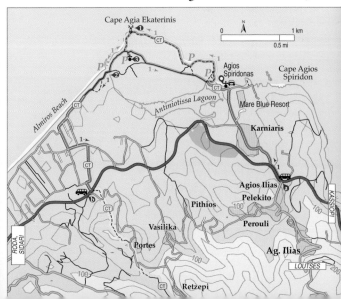

and you soon cross a small bridge over a tidal stream. This very pretty spot, overlooking the lagoon to the inland hills, is quite untypical of Corfu. Immediately over the bridge, by the rail, descend to the right, to head along the edge of the water, which is the lagoon's first outlet to the sea. (But if it's high tide, you will have to continue along the gravel road for a few metres, then follow the slightly-overgrown path that strikes off into the scrub, curving slowly to the right to return to the shoreline.)

Once at the water's edge, pick up a path heading round the promontory. A ribbon of pale green water borders the limestone shoreline. Within the first **20min** you're crossing the first cove, one of my favourite places to picnic. But don't plan to swim here: a bar of rocks cuts across this cove near the shore. Rejoin the coastal path at the far

View inland from the lagoon's second outlet to the sea — a lovely picnic spot, but without shade

end of the beach. Quite different from the area not far to the south, this coastline is flat and bare of trees. Inland, the massive mound of Pantokrator bulges out of the landscape. Across the straights, in Albania, the coastal hills climb into mountains. The path continues around the coast, passing a BEACON at the tip of **Cape Ekaterinis** (❶; **35min**), the northernmost point on Corfu.

Heron

Terebinth trees encroach on the shoreline as you round the headland, and a second cove comes into sight. From here one can see straight along the coast as it curves towards Cape Astrakeri, and Roda doesn't seem very far away. The ruins of an old monastery are visible, in a clump of trees up ahead. A few minutes later you cross the SECOND COVE. Here you pick up a track which takes you to a JUNCTION: turn right. Crossing a small rise, you look down on some sea walls built of rock (probably to protect the outlet channel ahead); to the right is **Almiros Beach** — an endless stretch of sand. Minutes later come to the lagoon's second outlet to the sea (❷; **45min**), with a footbridge across to Almiros — another lovely picnic spot (see opposite). This is where the main walk turns back. *(For the Alternative walk, refer to the map to follow the Corfu Trail from here to the bus stop at the Portes turn-off, 35 minutes away; the turn-off is slightly to the right of where you meet the main road.)*

The main walk returns from the outlet to the junction, where you keep straight ahead. Barely 70m/yds beyond the junction, you come to a grove of eucalyptus on the right. Take the path (which may be somewhat overgrown) through the grove, to explore the ABANDONED MONASTERY (❸). But take care around the old walls and the steps: both have crumbled away in places.

Green lizard

Then return to the main track and follow it back to Ag Spiridon, ignoring all side-tracks. Beyond the monastery the way is briefly flanked by tall cypress trees, and avenues of pine lie behind them. It's a cool few minutes. Finally you cross an open, treeless flat area covered in ferns, before reaching **Ag Spiridon** (❍; **1h30min**).

Terrapin

Walk 2: ABOVE IMEROLIA

See map on reverse of touring map; see also photo page 17

Distance/time: 4km/2.5mi; at least 2h (see under grade)

Grade: ● moderate, but with a steep climb and descent on paths that may be *very* overgrown in spring and slippery when wet. Ascent/descent of 300m/1000ft

Equipment: walking boots, long socks, sunhat, suncream, long-sleeved shirt, fleece, raingear, picnic, water

Picnic: the flower-filled valley at the start of the walk

Access: 🚌 to/from Imerolia (park by the main road just east of the village (39° 47.251'N,

19° 54.735'E) or Ag Ilias/Loutses 🚌 to/from Imerolia (Timetable 11). Alight on the east side of the village, where a concreted track forks off left between a bus shelter and the first house on the left (coming from Kassiopi).

Alternative walk: ● distance/grade/access as main walk. You *could* descend to Kato Bodholakos and from there to the main road, then walk back to your car (*not* recommended; busy road) or *flag down* a bus (no bus stop) back to base. *Note: aggressive dogs have been seen at Kato Bodholakos, but not for the last few years.*

This walk is Kassiopi's best kept secret. Not only does it have one of the prettiest footpaths on the island, but in spring it's a garden full of colour. The whole route is drenched with flowers. And not only are there fine views on offer, but an isolated hamlet is an added bonus. Unfortunately an old footpath above the school we used in the past to make a circuit has been blocked off, so the walk is now out-and-back (the Alternative walk is *not* recommended). A short hike, this walk is ideal in the evening, when it's cooler and the light is at its best. Don't miss it.

The walk starts on the east side of the village of **Imerolia**. Head up a concreted track leading into the valley behind the village: the route begins next to the BUS SHELTER (○), 30m east of the Imerolia Taverna on the other side of the road. A minute or two along, after a chicken coop, turn left off the track (which continues over a stream bed), and ascend a path. The path is lined with a profusion of colourful flowers — a very pretty place to picnic. The valley floor, crammed with trees, is fresh and verdant; the valley walls lean back steeply on either side. The path crosses the stream bed (**7min**) and runs alongside the track, before

climbing more steeply up the left side of the valley. It then descends gently, passes through a shady tunnel of trees, and crosses the stream bed again. A minute later (**20min**), take the well-used stony path climbing steeply on the right. A strenuous climb lies ahead. Within minutes you pass through a little wood of kermes oaks, the path ascending in zigzags.

A couple of minutes further along, the path flattens out, and you pass alongside the remains of a STONE PEN (❶) on the left. The path forks from time to time, but soon joins up again. In spring you may be up to your midriff in vegetation! Now in the higher

Flower-filled Bodholakos

reaches of the valley, five-six minutes from the pen, leave the valley floor and ascend the low crest on the left, ignoring a path to the right (which leads to a well below an WALLED-IN OLIVE GROVE; ❷). Animal paths around here will confuse you but, if you walk in a curving arc to the left, in just one minute you should find yourselves to the right of another WALLED-IN OLIVE GROVE (❷). Remaining alongside the wall, continue up to the right, ignoring all paths forking off right.

Reaching the end of the wall, a short strip of concrete takes you to a farm track. Turn left to reach the large farmhouse. This is part of the tiny outpost of **Bodholakos** (**52min**), with well-tended vegetable plots and chicken coops. Continue up the two-wheeled track, passing to the left of the house. Another home-stead, equally large, appears behind it. And between the two, you'll find a lovely big oak tree to sit under and contemplate your peaceful surroundings and the

stupendous view. (But the best viewpoint is five minutes uphill.) To continue the walk, stand facing this SECOND HOUSE. There's a chicken pen and a small shed a few metres to the right of it. Between the pen and the shed is a large clump of rock on the hillside ahead. That's your target. Follow the path that ascends to the right of the little shed, keeping straight up and aiming for the right-hand side of the clump of rock. The path then swings left to ascend up over the CLUMP OF ROCK (❸; **1h**). Here's where you can pause for a while and soak up the magnificent panorama that lies before you, with the bare mountains of Albania filling in the backdrop. Just below you can see a corner of Kassiopi; to the right is Avlaki's bay and, behind that, the almost-hidden Lake Butrinto in Albania. Sitting here until late evening, under a softening sun, is therapeutic beyond words.

From here I suggest that you just retrace your steps. Those who will do anything to avoid an out-and-back walk *could* now descend via the lower farmhouse and continue down the gently descending track, with a superb panorama ahead. You will pass your ascent route on the right and, five minutes later an isolated farmstead on the left, **Kato Bodholakos** (**④**). Continue down the track, with the lovely views shown on page 17 opening up towards Kassiopi below to the right. Remains of stone walls are a prominent feature in the landscape, and the hillside is a mass of flowers in the spring. Further into the descent, you look across to Albania, with its bleak and arid mountains in the distance. Keep to this motorable track all the way to the main road, where you walk round a barrier (for motor traffic) and then flag down a bus — or walk the busy stretch 1.5km back east to your car (not recommended, as there is *no* pavement).

Walk 3: the Vlacharena Chapel by the Dandalo Mansion near the end of the walk; note the blue flash waymark on the chapel wall

Walk 3: ACHARAVI PANORAMA CIRCUIT

See map on reverse of touring map; see also photograph opposite

Distance/time: 11.5km/7.1mi; 4h15min

Grade: fairly strenuous; some steep ascents on stony paths; ascent/descent 500m/1640ft overall; blue waymarking throughout *(but pay attention!)*

Equipment: boots or stout shoes with good ankle support/grip, sunhat, sunglasses, suncream, long-sleeved shirt, long trousers, fleece, raingear, picnic, water

Picnic: track about 12min into the walk; **Moni Vlacharena or** Dandalo mansion near the end

Access: 🚌 or 🚙 to/from Acharavi; alight/park near the roundabout on the main road (39° 47.523'N, 19° 48.971'E)

Short walk: Circuit from Lafki. 2.3km/1.4mi; 45min. ● Easy; stout shoes will suffice. From the church walk west towards PETALIA for 250m, then turn right on a wide track. Rising just slightly, you round **Messovouno Hill** with wonderful views over the north coast. The track makes a circuit back to the church.

A user suggested this flower-filled 'panorama hike' to us last year — just in time for it to be included in this new edition. It has been brilliantly waymarked by a resident, with blue plastic markers on trees and telephone poles at strategic junctions, supplemented with blue paint flashes. *Pay attention* to the waymarks: the route can be easily missed at times!

Starting at the ROUNDABOUT in the centre of **Acharavi** (**O**), head west towards Roda on the main road. After 100m/yds, at a BLUE PLASTIC '8' WAYMARK WITH ARROW on a telephone pole at the right, turn left into the car park of the local TOWN HALL (with the flagpoles). You will follow BLUE ROUTE 8 up to Priftatika, the first village en route. Walk to the right of the town hall on a lane, shortly reaching the road to Episkopi. Turn left here for just 100m; then, at a Y-fork, go left *(not waymarked)*. Go left immediately on a driveway, thn immediately right on a two-wheel track (which will be very overgrown in spring). Shortly, go left on a path (blue plastic marker), cross a METAL FOOTBRIDGE, and bear left on the far side.

Your path now rises in zigzags, with the odd BLUE DOT marking the way as you skirt to the left of an olive grove. The shady path swings right to a grassy/stony track (**12min**), where you go left. Looking back, there is a good view over Acharavi and the coast. This is a very pretty picnic spot.

Once over a rise, you descends to a minor road/motorable track where you again head left. After about 200m a BLUE ARROW on a tree signals your right turn over a BRIDGE, from where you can see Priftatika on the hillside above. Go left at the Y-fork on the far side of the bridge (BLUE PLASTIC WAYMARK). Just over 500m into the climb (after about eight minutes) *watch for* your turn-off right on a path: there is no plastic marker, but there *is* a BLUE ARROW on a rock some metres along the path.

49

Winding uphill, the path ends at a BULLDOZED AREA below a chain link fence and olive grove. Follow the fence to the left (where it ends) and you will spot a BLUE PLASTIC WAYMARK ON A POLE. Turn left uphill on the track in front of the olive grove and go left again at a Y-fork in the track. Just 40 paces from this fork, *watch for* a BLUE ARROW on the ground and turn right up a path. This takes you up to some houses, where you turn left to the main village road in the **Priftatika** (❶; 1h).

Turn left on the road for 150m, then pick up BLUE ROUTE 4 on the left by some rubbish bins (BLUE PLASTIC MARKER ON A TREE at the right). The path descends steeply, crosses a FOOT-BRIDGE and rises to the CHURCH in **Ag Pandelimon** (❷; 1h40min). Keep right in front of the church and climb steps up to the village, where some fine old manorial houses, now crumbling or in disrepair, testify to past wealth. At the top you reach the narrow 'main road'. Turn right and zigzag uphill for about 1km, to where the road turns 90° right. A SHRINE on the left and a BLUE '4' WAYMARK on a telephone pole at the right now signal a 2000-year-old route the locals call the 'SECRET TRAIL' (❸), where you turn left, steeply uphill. Recently reopened by the Corfu Trail Trust, this was originally an escape route for the inhabitants of Ivi (Acharavi) who fled the coast in 30BC, when their settlement was destroyed by Octavius (they had made the mistake of siding with Anthony and Cleopatra, losers in the battle of Actium…).

This *kalderimi* (stone-laid track)

seems to end at a turning area, but it just narrows to a path and climbs a valley towards Panto-krator. Further up the trail has been bulldozed away: follow the track past an isolated farm and to a road in the hamlet of **Trimodi** (❹; 2h25min). Follow the road to the left for a few metres; then,

by the 'TRI-MODI' sign on the left and this little SHRINE on the right, turn left. Follow this track for 60m until, by a

Jerusalem sage enlivens the track round Messovouno Hill on a cloudy day.

tall cypress, a BLUE WAYMARK points you down a steep path on the right.

The path drops to a stony track rounding **Messovouno Hill**, which you now circle in a clockwise direction. Soon you will have a fine outlook over Corfu's north coast. To your left in the distance are the Diapon-tian Islands — with Puglia in southern Italy behind them; to your right is the Albanian coast, backed by high, perhaps snow-capped peaks. Roda and Acharavi are just below, straddling the long beach collaring St George's Bay.

You may wish to detour into **Lafki** for some refreshment — it's just a short way ahead — but the main walk turns left before the village, on a rough downhill track (**❺; 2h40min**) indicated by BLUE '4' WAYMARKS. Beyond an old WELL, the track ends abruptly and a narrow path follows on. Apparently locals call this 'THE NUN'S PATH', but we are not sure why... It delves into a wild primeval valley, full of floral colour in spring and autumn. But *take care:* it can be very slippery underfoot.

You emerge on the same 'main road' you left to climb the 'Secret Trail' (**❻; 3h15min**); the hamlet of **Vracheri** is just off to the right. Turn left for 400m, then turn right down a concreted lane (BLUE PLASTIC '4' ON A TELEPHONE POLE). Follow this down past scattered housing, to emerge on a crossing tarmac road.

Follow this narrow road to the *right* (away from Acharavi) for a little over 250m, then go left at a sign, 'ENOPIA' (**❼**). This track brings you to the chapel shown on page 48, **Moni Vlacharena** (**❽**). Almost beside it, to the left, is the ruin of the **Dandolo Mansion**, once the home of a noble Venetian family. BLUE WAYMARKS guide us along a path at the right of the fortress-like ruin and through the surrounding woods. Emerging from the woods, descend to a dirt track and turn right. Take the next BLUE-WAYMARKED turn to the left, cross a riverbed and

Left: this two-wheel track is a pleasant picnic spot under 15 minutes into the walk; behind are views to Acharavi. Above: the Dandalo Mansion

continue back to the narrow road you left earlier. Turn right. After 100m you *could* turn right uphill with the '4' WAYMARKS and follow a circuitous route back to your starting point, but our main walk simply follows this narrow road all the way back to the ROUNDABOUT in **Acharavi** (**○; 4h15min**).

Walk 4: CIRCUIT FROM NISSAKI

Nissaki • Rou • Porta • Vigla • Kouloura • Kalami • Kaminaki • Nissaki

See map on reverse of touring map

Distance/time: 12km/7.4mi; 4h20min

Grade: ● fairly strenuous, with a steady ascent of 350m/1150ft (1h15min) at the start, and a steep (slippery when wet) 30-minute descent back to sea level at Kouloura; thereafter quite easy. Some yellow waymarks

Equipment: boots or stout shoes with good ankle support/grip, sunhat, sunglasses, suncream, long-sleeved shirt, long trousers, fleece, raingear, swimwear, picnic, water

Picnic: above Katavolos (views); coves/beaches on the return

Access: 🚗 or Nissaki 🚌 to/ from Garnelatika, Nissaki's easternmost hamlet. Parking in Nissaki is difficult. Park carefully beside the main road — as close as possible to the access road to the Sunshine Corfu Hotel and Spa (identified by flagpoles in front; 39° 43.604'N, 19° 54.306'E). There may also be parking space on the side road that passes the hotel entrance. All the bus drivers know this stop; journey time 45min

Short/Shorter walks

1 Katavolos: 2.5km/1.5mi; 1h10min; ● moderate ascent of 200m/6500ft. An out-and-back walk to a lovely picnic spot: above the hamlet of Katavolos there are stunning sea views over the Gulf of Kerkyra and Albania.

2 Nissaki — Rou — Porta — Vigla — Kouloura: 8.6km/ 5.4mi; 3h10min. ● Grade/equipment/access as first part of main walk (to Kouloura). Return by 🚌 from the Kouloura/Kalami junction — back to Corfu town (journey time 55min) or back to your car at Nissaki (15min).

This satisfying circuit, partially waymarked with yellow dots and arrows, gives you a wonderful taste of north-east Corfu's hinterland and coast. You climb high above the rocky shores of Nissaki, up through the olive groves and out into the friendly tangle of trees and bushes that patch the rugged countryside. Superb views spill out all around you. Ensconced in these declining hills is the enchanting hamlet of Rou, with its beautifully designed holiday homes. Descending out of these isolated hills, enigmatic Albania is tantalizingly close — just a mile and a half away, across the straits. Coming down to Kouloura, we pass the white house where Lawrence Durrell wrote *Prospero's Cell.* Then we have a delightful and mostly easy coastal saunter back to the starting point.

The walk begins across the road from a PHARMACY and the SUNSHINE CORFU HOTEL AND SPA. The hotel, below the main road, is not visible, but look for a side road heading down to the coast: from the main road you can see the hotel's flagpoles (flags

52

a-flutter in season) and the entrance barrier. Climb the white crazy-paving steps just at the left of an ATM (cash dispenser; ❍). A minute uphill, just beyond an electricity pole on the left, your cobbled path rises to the right. Almost at once, head right again, crossing two water pipes. After a few metres, turn left, following the cobbled path uphill, passing very close to the left-hand side of a house. Some 100m further on, *take care:* turn off on a faint path to the right (it *may* be marked with yellow paint daubs). The way climbs steadily, and the path becomes more obvious. At a fork a few minutes later, go left, up a path bordered by stone walls.

Anywhere here above the houses, in the shade of olives trees, is pleasant for picnicking. A minute up from the fork, by a concrete water tank, ignore the path to the right (❶; part of the **CORFU TRAIL**). The next landmark, three minutes later, is a farm building in an olive grove off to the right. Head right at the fork 40m beyond the building and nearby electricity pole.

This was the charming scene which used to greet walkers entering Katavolos. Today these old pillars, no doubt built from the imitation marble quarried nearby, have been replaced by ugly concrete.

Meeting a TARMAC/CONCRETE ROAD (**35min**), follow it to the right uphill and rise into the hamlet of **Katavolos** (**②**) by turning right, off the road Keep up between the houses, catching views of Albania and Ipsos Bay, with Corfu Town behind it. The best views are still to come. Reaching the last houses, rejoin the road and follow it steadily uphill. The road reverts to gravel track. In a few minutes, where the track divides, be sure take the right-hand, descending, fork (**③**; marked by a wooden arrow when last surveyed). This concrete lane soon starts climbing gently, then reverts to a stone and earthen track, eventually giving superb unimpeded views across to Albania — a wonderful picnic spot. Low grey hills roll back to a high purple escarpment. Behind the hills, mirrors of blue betray the inland sea — Lake Butrinto. The only sign of civilisation comes from a green plain back in the hills.

Rounding the hillside, Porta comes into sight, loosely scattered on the ridge opposite. Rou, your immediate destination, soon appears at the top of the crest not far ahead. After passing the old QUARRIES (**1h15min**), keep ahead on this main track, *bypassing* **Rou** (**④**) to the east.* Then watch for an almost hidden path on the right, accompanied by a WATER PIPE and follow this downhill. Hemmed in by thick scrub, the path dips into the gully you've been rounding. Several minutes

---

*The owners of the very up-market Rou Estate have gated off the old footpath from Rou to Porta with a 'Private Footpath to Porta' sign.

downhill you cross a dry stream bed. Less than 10 minutes back uphill (just after crossing a water course), the path fades out, but just continue to follow the WATER PIPE straight uphill, and you will soon see the path again ahead of you. Two minutes later you're in **Porta** (**⑤**; **1h50min**). There's a café on the road where you emerge, but if it's mid-afternoon, the village will be deep in slumber…

Turn right and follow the road through Porta. Ignore the right turn signposted to Kendroma; follow the road to the left uphill, passing a BUS SHELTER on your right. Some 350/400m/yds beyond it, as the road swings left, turn right down a concrete drive. After just 8m/yds, bear left downhill on another concreted drive (unsigned). After about 80m/yds downhill (where the concrete drive curls round to the left to a house) take the path beside a well-made stone wall on the right. The path continues straight downhill between houses and emerges on the concrete lane you left earlier, which you now follow to the left downhill. Barely two minutes down, on a bend to the right, continue straight ahead, taking a path on the left.

Coming into **Vigla** (**⑥**; **2h05min**), join a concrete drive. Turn left downhill here, almost immediately reaching a T-junction where you turn right (near a defunct *cafeneion*, now a villa). Follow the road out of the village, as it swings first to the left and then right. Then take the third concrete drive turning off to the right, following it downhill *past* dark red Villa Astarti on the right. Continue straight down, keeping to the right of a stone wall. In spring the path may be overgrown, but it soon becomes more obvious, with the old cobblestone surface underfoot. The hillside is very steep; perfect for slipping on! Kalami Bay reappears through the olive trees, luring you down to its green and blue sea. Soon you step your way down onto a concrete drive leading to Vigla House. Cross the lane, with the villa's entrance gates immediately to your right, and drop steeply down a path (bearing left at the junction encountered almost immediately). Then descend a path on the right just past the swimming pool. Almost at once the path bears right, twisting down through olive trees. A few houses dot the hillside. The path drops down, with a galvanized water pipe running along the left side.

Joining a concrete road, follow this downhill overlooking the romantic little cove of Kouloura, neatly tucked into the neck of a headland. Just 100m/yds downhill, turn right down a path which leads past a large building signed 'TOWN HALL' to a refreshment kiosk on the ROAD TO KASSIOPI. Turn right for 200m/yds, then head left at the KOULOURA/KALAMI JUNCTION. Three minutes along, turn left downhill on a path. It quickly leads to **Kouloura** (**3h**). Have a break and perhaps a swim. *(Now the Shorter walk returns the same way for 10 minutes, to catch a bus at the junction on the main road.)*

After a break, the main walk continues from here back to Nissaki: walk along the coast, *reversing the first part of Walk 5* from point ❺ to point ❶. At the far end of **Kalami Beach** you pass the WHITE HOUSE where Lawrence Durrell wrote *Prospero's Cell*; it's now a restaurant. Follow the road up the hill, then turn left on a concrete lane and down a path, to reach the lovely cove of **Gialiskari** (**3h25min**), another pretty place to picnic — as is the chapel of **Ag Arsenious** shown on page 57. Continue along the coast path as far as **Kaminaki**, then take the steep concrete road leading up to the main coast road (where Walk 5 begins). Either catch the bus here (to return to Corfu Town) or turn left and walk 15 minutes along the road back to your car in **Garnelatika/ Nissaki** (❍; **4h20min**).

Gialiskari, the unspoilt cove beyond Kalami

Walk 5: COASTAL WALK NORTH OF NISSAKI

Nissaki • Kalami • Kouloura • Kerasia Beach • Ag Stefanos • Sinies

Map on reverse of touring map; see also photograph page 55

Distance/time: 10.3km/6.4mi; 3h35min

Grade: ●❖ easy as far as Kouloura. Beyond Kouloura there are some awkward stretches, with a possibility of vertigo. The detour to the chapel of Ag Arsenious is steep and rough: care is needed. Height gain no more than 100m/330ft. Road-walking beyond Kerasia Beach.

Equipment: walking boots or stout shoes with ankle support and good grip, sunhat, -glasses, -cream, long-sleeved shirt, long trousers, raingear, swimwear, picnic, water

Picnic suggestions: any cove or beach en route

Access: Nissaki 🚌 to the stop at Kaminaki, 200m east of the Shell petrol station; journey time 45min. Or 🚗: park near the bus stop (39° 43.842'N, 19° 54.657'E). Return by Kassiopi 🚌 from Sinies — back to Corfu Town (journey time 1h) or to your car at Nissaki (journey time 15min)

Short walk: Nissaki to Kouloura. 5.5km/3.5mi; 1h30min. ●❖ Easy; access/equipment as above, but stout shoes will suffice. *I heartily recommend this for beginners.* Follow the main walk to Kouloura and from there head up to the junction on the main road for a Kassiopi bus heading back to Corfu Town or Nissaki.

Alternative walk: Erimitis Nature Reserve. 8.5km/5.3mi; 2h30min. ● Easy; Kassiopi 🚌 to Sinies; return on 🚌 from Kassiopi. Or 🚗: park at the last taverna in Ag Stefanos (39° 46.053'N, 19° 56.913'E) and start there, then take a 🚌 from Kassiopi to Sinies and walk from there back to their car.) Start out by leaving the bus at **Sinies** (**⑨**). Walk 100m/yds down the road towards Ag Stefanos, to pass the Sinies Supermarket on your left. Then fork left on the road with the 'no through road' sign and, almost immediately, take the first sealed track on the left. Follow this to **Ag Stefanos** CHURCH (**⑧**) and turn right to the sea. Just before the MOST NORTHERLY TAVERNA (**⑦**) in the village you will come to an information board ('Natural Wildlife of Erimiti') with a route map on the left. (A nearby supermarket may have a guide to this small nature reserve in stock.) We've chosen to take the paths closest to the shore because the beaches are so lovely. You could just do an out-and-back or a circuit on quiet roads. Or walk on to **Avlaki Beach** (**ⓐ**; where there is a good taverna) and then continue on the quiet road to **Kassiopi** (**ⓑ**) for a bus back to Corfu Town or to Sinies to collect your car.

T his coastal walk winds its way in and out of Corfu's most beautiful coves. The magnetic charm of these seascapes will not allow you to escape with less than a full day's rambling and swimming.

The walk starts at the KAMINAKI BUS STOP (**⓪**). Take the steep concrete road leading down to the first cove, **Kaminaki** — a tourist hamlet with a touch of charm. Head left along the CORFU TRAIL, following the path up over the rocks at the end of

Looking across to the little chapel of Ag Arsenious

the beach (keep to the left of the concrete platform). Within the next five minutes, you cross **Nissaki Beach**, passing in front of the NISSAKI BEACH HOTEL. The path continues for 50m/yds above its volley ball court; ascend the steps at the centre of its grounds, almost to the front door, then head right to continue.

Rounding the hillside, and looking across the small cove shown above, you'll see the inconspicuous chapel of **Ag Arsenious** (❶) set in rock ahead. Soon after spotting the chapel, follow a green chain-link fence down towards the sea. (A nearby sign, 'Agni', indicates your onward path after visiting the chapel.) The three-minute descent is steep, slightly vertiginous and rocky, but it's a pretty spot (another lovely picnic spot). Swimming off the rocks here is great fun, too.

After your visit retrace steps to continue along the **CORFU TRAIL** which climbs some stone steps and soon turns sharp right onto a wide earth and stone track with a concrete wall on its seaward side. At a junction of tracks, head slightly uphill to the left towards another flight of stone steps. Climb these, follow a short level section of path, then drop down another flight. Having rounded this development, you now rejoin the path, still following the coast.

Keep straight on to the next cove, **Agni** (❷; **40min**). A minute along, near the end of the beach, pick up the path again, just beyond a concrete driveway. Minutes along, fork right off the main path, to follow the shore, where lovely smooth rocks slope down into the water — natural bathing platforms. The beach, **Gialiskari**, shown on page 55, is deserted and naked of buildings — quite a surprise since, by late morning (in peak season), the horizon is dotted with boats converging on this cove-indented coastline, like a flotilla of junks seeking shelter from a typhoon. There is a concrete shed at the point where you first come on to this deserted beach. To continue to the next 'cove of call', Lawrence Durrell's beloved Kalami, head up the dry stream bed at the right of this shed. Half a minute along, bear right, heading between fenced-in plots. Ignore the branch-off to the left a minute along; keep uphill on a concrete lane. Bear right along the lane, which soon becomes tarmac. **Kalami Beach** is just around the bend; unfortunately, an apartment complex now scars this once-idyllic little cove. The lovely large restaurant building you step past was DURRELL'S HOME (**3**) in his *Prospero's Cell* days. Take the steps down to the beach. At the end of the beach, beyond the last taverna, follow a path up to the road.

The main walk now makes for Kouloura, a little over 10 minutes away. (But between the two bays there are some exquisite swimming spots off the limestone shelves. To reach them, turn off the road about seven minutes along: the fairly steep and narrow path turns off immediately past the last house on the right.) Following the road, continue straight on at the junction, ignoring the turn-off to the left. You descend to the idyllic little HARBOUR OF **Kouloura** (**4**; **1h10min**), in the shade of tall cypresses. Overlooking a small pier sheltering fishing vessels, this is probably one of the most photographed spots on the island. (*From here, those doing the Short walk should return to the*

junction and ascend to the main road.)

Leaving the small harbour behind, walk back up the road for a minute and then follow the lane straight ahead and down to Kouloura's quiet PEBBLE BEACH (**5**), shaded by tall eucalyptus trees. Just beyond the large derelict building at the end of the beach, climb the headland. Rounding a grassy hillside, reach COVE NUMBER SEVEN — a tiny stony beach tucked into the headland opposite Kouloura. Metres along this beach, climb the hillside to rejoin your path. About 25 minutes from Kouloura, you cross another beach — **Kerasia** (**6**; **1h40min**), a large and relatively unspoilt cove, again shaded by eucalypts. Pass the taverna at the end of the beach and meet a road. While there *is* a way along the coast ahead, passing the Rothschild villa, past users have found it dangerous. So turn right here and follow the road to the charming inlet of **Ag Stefanos** (**2h50min**). It has become another victim of tourism, but still retains a good portion of its original rustic flavour.

Keep along the road, past the LAST TAVERNA (off to the right; **7**). When the road makes a hairpin bend to the right, go straight ahead, on the gravel track to the left of the CHURCH (**8**). At a fork after 350m/yds, go left. After another 1km, ignore a turn-off right. Keep straight on, passing to the left of **Sinies** SUPERMARKET and rising to the BUS STOP on the main road (**9**; **3h35min**), where you can catch the Kassiopi bus on its way back to Nissaki and Corfu Town.

Walk 6: FROM NISSAKI TO LAFKI VIA ANO PERITHIA

Nissaki • Rou • Porta • Mengoulas • Ano Perithia • Lafki

See map on reverse of touring map; see also photo page 62
Distance/time: 16.6km/10.3mi; 5h20min
Grade: ● strenuous, with an overall ascent of 600m/1970ft; only recommended for experienced walkers. Snakes are not uncommon in this terrain. Follows waymarked CORFU TRAIL for much of the way
Equipment: walking boots, long socks, jacket/fleece, sunhat, sunglasses, suncream, long-sleeved shirt, long trousers, raingear, picnic, plenty of water
Picnic suggestions: anywhere en route, especially Old Perithia
Access: 🚗 Motorists see Walk 7 on page 62 for a circular walk. 🚌 to Garnelatika (as for Walk 4 on page 52); journey time 45min. Return on 🚌 from Lafki (only one departure Mon-Fri at 15:30; *recheck this departure time before setting out!*).

If you're an experienced walker and don't mind crossing some rough ground, this is a fantastic hike. You cross the vast flanks of Pantokrator, where the shepherd roams with his flocks and herds of goats … and occasionally the hunter roams with his gun. Rustic hamlets and villages lie en route; in between, rocky hillsides slide down into sheer, narrow valleys. Following the faintest of paths — and often just your nose, you trail through the loneliest landscape on the island. The countryside is undeveloped (in the best possible sense of the word) and rich in flora. With its striking panoramas, this walk lacks for nothing.

Start out by following WALK 4 (page 52) as far as **Porta** (❺; **1h50min**). When you reach the road on the outskirts of Porta, where Walk 4 turns right, turn left, soon passing a large CHURCH on the right.* Three minutes above the church, turn right at a junction. Judas trees lie off the route. In spring their rich pink-to-mauve flowers hang in clusters off their leafless branches — a splendid sight. Tradition has it that this is the tree on which Judas Iscariot hung himself after denouncing Christ and, according to legend, the once-pale flowers turned pink in shame.
Mountainous Albania stretches out before you, and Lake Butrinto is visible, although partially hidden behind the coastal hills. The tiny lighthouse island of Peristator lies off Cape Varvara. Santa is the small village two ridges away. Looking up the road, you spot Mengoulas — your immediate destination. This hamlet perches high on a hillside knoll.
A good 10 minutes along the road turn left up a concrete lane into **Mengoulas** (❻; **2h20min**). Follow the road round to the right, to a very attractive paved area refurbished with EU money by the restored 'Thresher's

*Just 50m/yds past this church the CORFU TRAIL takes a woodland path to Santa before heading on to Mengoulas. You may prefer this pretty route, which adds 1km to the walk.

59

House' (a tourist villa). The road then curves round to the left and the tarmac surface reverts to a rough track; a deep ravine runs parallel to the track, on your right. Some 300m/yds along, at a T-junction with another track, turn left. At the next junction (after about 700m/yds), go straight ahead uphill. A long, steady climb up this wide track (part of the **CORFU TRAIL**) will bring you to the high pass in about 35 minutes, all the time providing you with views down over the Kerkyra Gulf and across the straits to Albania.

On the PASS (**❼**; **3h**) there's a small tiled-roofed open-sided SHELTER with picnic table and benches, where you can take a break and admire the views. (*Walks 8b-c and 9 join here.*) At this stage you can also identify most of the initial descent route to Ano Perithia. Below you, to the north, you will see a shallow green valley with a few terraced fields and a low, roofless, STONE RUIN (**❽**). You are aiming to walk down towards this ruin and 60

then to pass through a steeper valley leading out of its left (western) end. Just at the right of the shelter, take the clear, flower-filled CAIRNED PATH down to the left making straight for the ruin. In the later stages of the descent there are more cairns as the way heads through bracken. Some 100m/yds short of the ruin, the path turns left into a dry stream bed and merges with an old path coming from the right. Follow this steeply downhill, keeping to the left side of a steep and narrow gully. The pleasant sound of ringing bells alerts you to flocks of sheep and herds of goats, but pinpointing them amongst all this rock is another thing! Wild pears are the only trees hardy enough to survive in this rocky terrain.

Ano Perithia begins to unravel, building by building. Keep descending, wending your way between rocky outcrops. The path, not always obvious, is marked with cairns and some yellow paint dots on boulders. Continue carefully down until

Left: on the descent to Ano Perithia; above: archway in the village

you join a track near a WATER COLLECTION TANK on the right. (This is the track to Lafki, which you will follow later.) Turn left on the track, and then take the next track downhill to the right, just before a CHURCH. When you reach the bottom of a flight of steps leading up to the church, fork right down a cobbled path which passes between the old village houses. In two minutes you cross a gully next to a re-roofed CHAPEL, and then briefly ascend to **Ano Perithia** (ⓐ; **3h 40min**), where you can refuel at one of the tavernas in the main square or picnic in the shade of trees or buildings. Ano Perithia was once a thriving community with grand houses and six churches. Restoration is under-way, and a new water supply has been installed. The houses are being bought and restored by the wealthy. Fortunately the village has been declared a Heritage Site by the Greek government, so all work must conform to strict regulations. *(Walk 7 leaves along the track at the right of the village*

information board; Walks 8b and 9 leave along Loutses road at the left of the rose-coloured church.)
After a break, head back through the village to the Lafki track above the church and turn right. You will follow this track all the way to Lafki. From the opposite side of the valley, you have an excellent view back over Ano Perithia. Notice the interesting hill formation below the track, resembling a pack of propped-up cards. An hour from Perithia, you round the nose of a ridge and pass above lush pastures. A large abandoned dwelling sits above the track a little further on, and a deserted hamlet hides in the trees above. A colony of beehives occupies a level field on the right of the track below the house. Soon you're overlooking an impressive valley scarred by a large quarry. Lafki lies on the far side of it. You enjoy a good coastal view of Acharavi and the landscapes of Walk 3. Emerging on a road, turn left to **Lafki**. The BUS SHELTER (ⓑ; **5h20min**) is in the centre, by the CHURCH.

61

Walk 7: CIRCUIT TO OLD PERITHIA

**Map on reverse of touring map;
see also photos pages 60-61
Distance/time:** 13km/8mi;
4h15min
Grade/Equipment: ● as Walk 6
on page 59
Picnic suggestion: anywhere en
route, once off road

Access: 🚌 to/from Ag Martinos.
Park beside the road at the Lafki/
Perithia junction (39° 47.374'N,
19° 50.924'E) — the lowest point
in the walk, to get almost all the
climbing over early in the day.
But you could choose to park at
other points en route.

Walk 6 has been a favourite among hillwalkers for
many years, but these days people are more likely
to hire cars and prefer circular walks. This satisfying
circuit, with a descent along the Corfu Trail, is ideal for
motorists — but it's still strenuous!

Start out at the northern edge
of **Ag Martinos**; from the
LAFKI/PERITHIA JUNCTION (**O**)
walk up the road towards
'LAFKI 2KM', past the handful
of attractive houses that

comprise **Psachnia**. About 15
minutes later, just before
entering **Lafki**, a discreet blue
sign at the left announces your
track to 'OLD PERITHIA' (**❶**;
40min): it's surfaced at the
outset. It's a bit early in the
walk to be looking for refreshments, but you may like to
know that refreshments are
available in Lafki (**ⓑ**), just a
minute or two ahead.
The route now is very straightforward: you follow this track
— Walk 6 in reverse — all the
way to **Ano Perithia** (**ⓐ**;
2h30min), described in more
detail in Walk 6.
From here we take the CORFU
TRAIL downhill: it leaves from
the right of the VILLAGE MAP
('OLD PATH TO KRINIAS').
When the track runs out, keep
ahead on the path beneath
oaks, at the edge of a narrow
valley. After a steepish stretch,
the path zigzags down to cross
a dry river bed and rises up the
far side to a lane. Keep ahead,
then fork left, to emerge in
Krinias (**❷**; **4h05min**). From
here it's well under 1km by
road back to the junction in
Ag Martinos (**O**; **4h15min**).

Ano Perithia

Walk 8: THREE TOUGH HIKES FROM NISSAKI VIA PALIES SINIES (PALIO CHORIO)

See map on reverse of touring map; see also photographs on pages 2, 35, 60-61, 62, 72
Distance/time, Grade, Return transport: see Walks a-c below
Equipment: walking boots, sunhat, sunglasses, suncream, long-sleeved shirt, long trousers, fleece, jacket, raingear, swimwear (for Walks a and b), picnic, water
Access: 🚌 to Nissaki: ask to alight at the road to Viglatouri; journey time 45min

Picnic suggestion/Out-and-back for motorists: Palies Sinies.

10km/6.2mi; 3h. ● Moderate climb/descent of 220m/720ft on tracks, but *long*. 🚗 Park above Viglatouri, for instance near Villa Signalo (39° 43.925'N, 19° 53.298'E). Walk to Palies Sinies and back.

Walk a: Nissaki to Roda

Distance/time: 27km/16.7mi; 7h20min

Grade: ● strenuous; climb and descent of about 800m/2625ft. Only fit walkers should attempt the entire hike. Most of way follows tracks, but there are two short sections of pathless ascent up rocky slopes.
Return: 🚌 from Roda (journey time 1h). If you cut short the

hike, there are buses from Strinilas (Mon-Sat; journey time 1h20min) or Episkepsis (Mon-Sat; journey time 1h30min)

Shorter walk: Strinilas to Roda. 9.5km/6mi; 3h10min. ● Easy; all downhill on tracks — but steep and with some loose stones underfoot. Access: Lafki 🚌 to Strinilas; return as above. Pick up the walk at Strinilas (**6**; see page 66).

Walk b: Nissaki to Kalamaki

Distance/time: 20km/12.4mi; 5h50min

Grade: ● strenuous ascent of 680m/2230ft; only for experienced walkers. Some pathless sections both up and down steep rocky terrain
Return: Kassiopi 🚌 from Kalamaki Beach to Kassiopi, then change buses for Corfu Town (journey time 1h30min)

Walk c: Nissaki to Porta

Distance/time: 16km/10mi; 4h20min

Grade: ● strenuous climb and descent of 680m/2230ft, but mostly along tracks. Some clambering over rocky terrain
Return: 🚌 from Porta to Corfu Town; journey time 1h10min

All three versions of this hike begin by scaling the harsh, rock-smeared slopes of Pantokrator. On route you detour to the ruins of Palies Sinies (also known as Paleo Chorio) — a medieval village normally seen only from the summit of Pantokrator. The greenery that envelopes it betrays its presence in this stark hilly landscape. Every crest you master reveals spectacular views.

Alight from the bus at the ROAD TO VIGLATOURI (two minutes past Glyfa Beach, as the bus enters **Nissaki**). In case your driver does not know this stop, watch for the Glyfa Taverna on the right, and press the stop

button on the next seaward-curving bend. **Begin all three hikes** by heading up the road opposite the bus stop (**O**); it is signposted to VIGLATOURI, and there is a BUS SHELTER on the right. The steep climb up this

Palies Sinies (also known as Paleo Chorio); the church and bell tower have been restored.

tarred road is mitigated by the wonderful views. With every turn you're overlooking the glorious Kerkyra Gulf through olive trees, with the Albanian coastline in one direction and Ipsos Bay in the other. The shimmering sea lies like a plate of glass, with not a ripple to be seen. Soon a shoulder of Pantokrator rises on the far side of a ravine; Barbati Beach lies below.

Most of the steep road up to Viglatouri is lined with beautifully sited holiday villas. About 30 minutes up from the coast road, as you enter the hamlet of **Viglatouri** (❶), ignore a turning to the right. Keep ahead, passing VILLA ANTIGONE on the left and VILLA HELENA on the right. Five minutes (350m) uphill from this junction, after passing through olive groves and rounding a long S-bend, take a short cut: turn left on another road, then take a steep cobbled path ascending to the right between two houses. You join a concrete drive at VILLA SIGNALO, where you continue uphill. (The out-and-

back walk for motorists starts around here — or even higher up.)

Rejoining the tarmac road at the top of the drive, bear slightly left uphill. The road now reverts to concrete. A few minutes up, leave the olive groves behind and come onto a hillside fresh with grass. Heavy sprinklings of yellow-blooming broom lie below. Through the sheer ravine walls the coastline unravels. On fine days Corfu Town and the airport lagoon are picture-postcard clear and, beyond, the dark blue tail of the island is visible.

At a T-junction, turn left for Palies Sinies. Now on the CORFU TRAIL, we have to follow this road around the contours almost all the way to our destination; it has obliterated a lovely OLD STONE-LAID PATH (❷) which crossed the valley sooner and saved a good 2km of contouring.* But the views are superb, with the radiant blue gulf, framed by the ravine walls, capturing your attention. Heading deeper into the valley, you round a bend and see the ruined buildings of an old village up ahead. Fork right on another track just below the ruins, then follow a path off the end of the track and curve round to the right up through the ruins of **Palies Sinies** (❸; also known as

*This old path (❷; dotted line on our map) was the route of the Corfu Trail. If you see *fresh* yellow waymarks it *may* have been cleared and you might chance it. Otherwise be aware there are snakes hiding in the lacerating valley scrub.

Paleo Chorio; **2h10min**). You pass the shell of a large old house, with a stone table outside. Where better to take a lunch break? This old village is an intriguing place to explore, but do so with the utmost care, as some of the buildings could be in a dangerous state of decay. At least the church and its belltower have been restored. Not far past the house with the table are the old wells, on either side of the path. The water is drinkable, but be careful when drawing it up; the well is very old and the rocks built across the top of it are not secure. Beware also, during high summer, of hordes of wasps. Draw the water quietly. *(The Picnic suggestion/Out-and-back for motorists turns back here.)*

Leaving Palies Sinies involves a bit of scrambling; there is no path. Bear in mind that you are aiming for the track above the village. Standing between the WELLS, with your back to the village, ascend the hillside on your immediate left — making first for the church on the crest above (and slightly behind you). From the church head up the crest to the track. It's a steady climb up through the remains of terracing and scrub.

Reaching the track, turn right and follow it for about half an hour, up to a PASS (④; **2h50min**). If you're not being battered by the winds, plonk yourself down and soak up this magnificent panorama. To the north, down through the V in the hills, an another-deserted village is visible — Ano Perithia (Walks 6, 7, 8b, 9), with the mountainous interior of Albania in the back-

Alley in Episkepsis (Walk a)

ground. *(Walk a turns left at the T-junction here; Walks b and c turn right.)*

Walk a: Having turned left at the T-junction and passed a smelly livestock SHED, within 20 minutes you reach the PANTO-KRATOR ROAD. If you haven't already seen the monastery (⑤; photograph page 72), it's less than 30 minutes uphill (a detour *not* included in the overall times). Continuing to the right, you cross a vast plateau, weaving your way around sharp rocky mounds of rock. Sunken, grass-lined hollows create green water-less lakes. This is goat country. A little further on, the north coast appears, with a view over Cape Astrakeri. The return to civilisation comes when you catch sight of the small country village of Petalia below the road. Fifty minutes down from the Pantokrator junction, you emerge on another ROAD. Turn left and, five minutes later, enter **Strinilas** (⑥; **4h20min**) — by the pretty village square, shaded

by a gargantuan elm tree. If you feel you've done enough today, you can catch a bus here. *(This is also where the Shorter version of Walk a begins.)*

Just beyond the square, and immediately after the sign denoting the edge of the village, turn right down a concrete lane. At the T-junction 30m/yds ahead, turn left down a track which will take you to the doorstep of Episkepsis. On the way you'll spot Ag Triada, the magnificently-sited monastery visited in Walk 10, perched on the highest hill in the north. The route drops down into a concealed combe before crossing a shelf of fallow plots. Winding down through olive groves, come down onto a ROAD (**5h20min**). Turn left uphill, entering a charming archetypal farming community. Take the first turn-off right down an alley flanked by houses, to pass by a CHURCH. Keep downhill and, at the junction, descend another alley to the left, to the main road in the centre of **Episkepsis** (**7**; **5h30min**). Notice the charming three-storied Venetian manor on the right here.

Turn left on the main road; you will come to three cafés. (If you're winding up the walk here, the BUS STOP is 30m/yds beyond these cafés, before the sharp bend.) The final leg of the main hike begins by one of the cafés — the ELLINIKON, with POST BOX outside. Head down the road alongside it, passing another CHURCH and the SCHOOL within a minute. Continue on through a severed arm of the village, spread along a ridge below the main settlement. Beyond the houses, pass a CONCRETE WELL and

SHRINE and ignore a fork to the left. The lane gives way to a narrow farm track as you descend through old olive groves. About 10 minutes from the village, at a fork, ignore the track which snakes steeply downhill to the right. Climb up to the left, rounding the shoulder of a ridge, then drop down into a deep, shady valley on the far side. It's very pretty countryside; the valley floor displaying a rich assortment of foliage.

You cross a small BRIDGE and, gradually, the hills fold back to disclose a boat-shaped valley. Recross the stream several minutes later. A minute after this stream crossing, join a track coming from the right and follow it to the left, along the opposite side of the valley. Oaks make a brief appearance, then a pleasant grassy patch appears below the track. Leaving these abrupt valleys behind, your way begins opening out. A little over 10 minutes from the last stream crossing, ignore a faint track branching off to the right and, two minutes later, another track forking off right. Wending your way through the valley floor, you reach the coastal plain.

Coming to a tarmac road, turn left. In a couple of minutes, having crossed a bridge over a stream, you reach a road on the outskirts of **Sfakera** (**6h50min**). Turn right towards Roda. Thirty minutes along, after crossing straight over the main coast road, you'll come to **Roda**'s beach. The BUS STOP (**9**; **7h20min**) is where the road meets the sea — on the left side of the road, north of the junction.

Walk b: Having turned right at the T-junction, in three minutes you reach an small open-sided SHELTER with picnic table and benches (waypoint **7** of Walk 6 on the map). Now follow the notes for Walk 6 from the 3h-point (page 60), to descend to **Ano Perithia**, and from there pick up Walk 9 at the 3h55min-point (page 71) to go on to **Kalamaki Beach**. (Or descend the Corfu Trail down to Almiros Beach and then walk on to Acharavi for a bus, but check scheduling in advance — Kalamaki buses are a safer bet outside the 'season'.)

Walk c: Having turned right at the T-junction, in three minutes reach an OPEN-SIDED SHELTER (waypoint **7** of Walk 6 on the map) and a track junction. Here turn right for Porta. At the next junction, 35 minutes later, head right — but, before you do so, continue on for another minute or so for stunning views over Porta to Albania. Just below the junction, pass a shed and take the fork to the left. Thirty minutes downhill, turn right for **Porta** (**5** on the map), a good five minutes away. Pick up the BUS at the TURNABOUT/PARKING AREA in the village.

Walk c: on the descent to Porta, with Albania in the distance

Walk 9: TAXIARKHIS CHAPEL AND NORTH ALONG THE CORFU TRAIL

Spartilas • Mount Pantokrator • Ano Perithia • Loutses • Kalamaki Beach

Out-and-back for motorists
See map on reverse of touring map
Distance/time: 3km/2mi; 1h30min
Grade: ●: moderate-strenuous, with ascents and descents of about 280m/920ft; one short vertiginous stretch; All Corfu Trail waymarked
Equipment: stout shoes or boots, sunhat, long trousers, picnic, water
Picnic suggestion: above Spartilas or Taxiarkhis chapel
Access: 🚌 to/from Spartilas, park as close as possible to the church where the walk starts (see text below; 39° 43.251'N, 19° 50.428'E)

Linear hike for bus users
See map on reverse of touring map; see also photographs pages 60-61, 62 and 72
Distance/time: 19.5km/12mi; 5h55min
Grade: ●: very strenuous, with an ascent of about 600m/1970ft and descent of 906m/2970ft. For experienced walkers only. Short stretches of path are partially overgrown, and one short stretch is vertiginous. It is very rocky on top of the plateau; take your time. Do not attempt in bad weather or when there is low cloud. Corfu Trail waymarked as far as Old Perithia
Equipment: walking boots, sunhat, sunglasses, suncream, long-sleeved shirt, long trousers, raingear, swimwear, picnic, water, plenty of insect repellent in summer (when there are flies galore)
Picnic suggestions: above Spartilas, Taxiarkhis chapel
Access: any 🚌 to Pyrgi/Ipsos (30min) and taxi from there to the village centre in Spartilas. (There is also a Spartilas bus, but it doesn't give enough time for the walk.) Return on Kassiopi 🚌 from Kalamaki Beach to Kassiopi; change buses for Corfu; journey time 1h30min

Spartilas is magnificently sited on the upper slopes of Pantokrator. No other village on the island commands such a view. And this ascent to a frescoed chapel, via a superb picnc setting with even finer views, is a perfect — if slightly strenuous — leg stretcher during Car tour 1.

But we've not forgotten those of you who shun car hire in favour of buses … and are up for a real challenge. This hike invites you to spend a day on the inhospitable slopes of Pantokrator — clambering up animal paths, pushing your way through scrub and floundering over rocks. No walk on the island offers so much adventure, or discomfort. From the summit (906m/2970ft), your views stretch as far south as Paxos and Antipaxos and — on rare occasions — to the toe of Italy. What one remembers most, however, is the captivating view of neighbouring Albania. Ano Perithia, Corfu's most isolated village, rests in a hollow of trees not

Frescoes in the chapel of Taxiarkhis

far below, girded by buffer hills of bright grey rock. We take a break there before descending to the north coast.

Ask your taxi driver to drop you at the pretty yellow café in the centre of **Spartilas** (⦿), with a large CocaCola sign and post box outside. (The bus stops here.) **Start off** with your back to the café: walk left (west) until you see a CHURCH at the right of the road raised above a retaining wall. (This is *not* the church with flagpoles on the main village street near the café.) Two alleys head up right before the church: take the right-hand (narrower) alley, climbing up between hillside houses. There is a YELLOW CORFU TRAIL DOT above some steps at the right. Less than half a minute up, behind the church, take the steps up to the left (YELLOW CORFU TRAIL ARROW at the top of the steps). Follow the concrete lane at the top of the steps uphill. It becomes a track. Three minutes up from the road, on a bend, leave the track and continue straight ahead on a path (the first turn-off you reach). Despite the Corfu Trail way-

markings, the first few minutes across these hillside plots are convoluted and require *attention*. You pass above an uninhabited house a minute from the turn-off. When the path forks, keep left (continuing in the same direction). Then ignore a faint turn-off left. Four minutes from the track, the path abruptly swings up to the left between stone walls in varying stages of decay. It then veers back to the right again, gradually ascending above olive groves — an ideal place to picnic, with views over Ipsos Bay — and heading along the foot of the escarpment. This much narrower path (with a very short vertiginous stretch), hemmed with vegetation, climbs all the way to the top of the plateau and the road to the Pantokrator summit.

Rounding a side-valley, you pass a ROCK (**15min**) jutting out from this scrub-covered slope; from here you have a foretaste of the panorama to come once you've reached the top. Bushes of

69

holm oak, *Pistacia lentiscus*, spiny broom, heather and Jerusalem sage hem you in, and the path is littered with empty shotgun cartridges. Approaching the plateau, the terrain becomes rockier. Clumps of heather, with purple and pink flower-heads, stand out on the hillside. Shiny-leafed strawberry trees begin appearing.

On reaching the PLATEAU (**45min**), branch off right to the CHAPEL OF **Taxiarkhis** (**❶**), barely a minute along. The path to it ascends through the remains of terracing. Holm oak bushes conceal the chapel, which stands just at the edge of the plateau. From here there is a spectacular panorama over the sweeping blue bays bitten out of the coastline. Stretching out before you, the island rises into a portly midriff, before tapering off into an undulating tail. And you have a bird's-eye view down onto Spartilas. This is the place to break out the picnic if you have brought one, and to take in the peaceful surroundings. But perhaps you will be as dismayed as I was to find the chapel door ajar, the roof falling in, and the exquisite wall and altar frescoes left to the ravages of nature … and man. Apparently the owners live in Athens (many chapels on the island are privately owned) and have no interest in restoration, while the Church — even if they were interested — can't afford it these days.

From here motorists return the same way down to their cars in **Spartilas** (**❍**; **1h30min**). Hardy souls heading on to Perithia and Kalamaki should first verify your ongoing route from behind the chapel. The way is through the very slight, bush-filled valley that heads directly towards Pantokrator (with the very obvious communications masts). Back on the well-marked path, keep straight ahead. Thyme and spiny broom layer the gently-subsiding inclines. Five minutes from the chapel, just after climbing the remains of a terraced bank, the path fades. Keep straight ahead, bearing right towards the valley. A minute later, pass through an intersection, to see a STONE BUILDING (**❷**; **55min**) just below the path. A path off to the right at the building takes you to a beautiful stone-laid WHEAT THRESHING FLOOR hidden in the trees. It's a very pretty spot. Ignore all the paths striking off uphill and out of the valley. Your way burrows through the scrub lining the V in the slope. At intervals, terraced plots appear through the bushes on the right. In summer this shady path which tunnels its way through holm oaks, provides a welcome break from the hot sun; in spring moss cushions the rock.

About 10 minutes from the stone building, you leave the oak forest. The path becomes rougher and enters a gully. Continue up the floor of the gully. You will notice a track above you: when TRAIL JOINS THE TRACK (**❸**), follow it to the right, then leave the track on the outside of a sharp bend by turning left. The footpath you now follow is a continuation of the gully. Grazing animals have made several paths in this area; keep to the main Corfu Trail, climbing up small terraces. Five minutes above the track, you reach another, higher level in the

Moni Pantocrator: the photographer has managed to edit out all the communications masts!

plateau. A grass-covered plain leads up to a choppy sea of rocky hummocks rising and falling all round. Beyond this unruliness lies Mt Pantokrator. Follow the waymarking: in summer, within seconds of entering the dry grass, flies will descend on you by the thousands, trying to crawl into every orifice laid open to them. Don't even cough, it's too risky! The bright side of this onslaught is that — tired though you may be — you certainly quicken your pace! *(If at this stage cloud or bad weather threaten, do not attempt to go further!)*

A couple of minutes across this extensive flat area swing left, following a slight depression. You briefly leave the grassy plots and head across a rock-strewn plain. Then the way becomes like an obstacle course, as you climb in and out of sunken pastures amidst this mass of rock. *Keep your eye on the waymarking*; it's easy to head off in the wrong direction! *Ignore* all the lettering waymarks; *follow* the arrows and dots. Small, long-stemmed *Euphorbia myrsinites* grows up here amidst the rock, and in

autumn golden-headed thistles *(Pallenis spinosa)* cover the rocky slopes. Closer to Pantokrator the mounds become sharper and the hollows deeper.

Crossing a crest, the mountain road comes into sight. From here on, if the waymarking has faded or become infrequent, just make for the road. Descending, remains of an old path appear. Dip down into a large valley cutting across in front of you. Bear left along it and, when you reach a double terraced wall, pick up a clear path ascending to the Pantokrator road, opposite a large CONCRETE WATER TANK (❹; **2h**).

Turn right, making for the summit and the monastery, passing a pretty shaded hillside hollow. A little further on, you're overlooking Ano Perithia, a haven of greenery, swallowed up by a mass of tumbling, rocky slopes — a welcoming sight in this bleak landscape. Passing under the belfry, you enter the grounds of **Moni Pantokrator** (❺; **2h25min**). Despite the juxtaposition of the beautifully restored chapel and a veritable

backdrop of glimmering sea and the enormous shadowy mountains of Albania. (If you're leaving here, the BUS STOP is at a junction at the far end of the village, just before a taverna/café.)

Those bound for Kalamaki Beach, however, turn up the first road branching off right, sign-posted to ANAPAFTIRIA. As you pass through a small cluster of houses, keep right at the first fork (a minute along), and left at the second (three minutes later), following the road.

At the end of the road lies the tiny village of **Anapaftiria** (**4h55min**). From here follow the wide track that continues on past the houses. Two minutes down, you're looking across the cerulean sea to Albania. This marvellous view remains with you for the rest of the hike. The track zigzags lazily down to the sea. There are no turn-offs. Sea squill, a lovely sight with its flowering white stem, is sprinkled liberally across the hillside. Nearing the sea, *Cardopatium corymbosum* — a tall thistle with clustered flowerheads — competes with mullein stalks for height.

Sandy Kalamaki Beach appears over to the left. Soon after, the track enters a scattering of bushes and laurels. Ignore a track off left. Fifty minutes downhill you meet the road, just above **Seki Bay** (**5h45min**), a pretty little cove concealed by cypress trees. There is a small taverna (not always open, unfortunately) on the main road. If you stop here, allow *at least* 10 minutes to reach your bus stop. It's to the left, by a café just before **Kalamaki Beach** (**5h55min**).

forest of towering communications masts, this is a truly magical setting. There is a café as well.

Descend the road from the monastery and take the first track off to the right. Follow this track for the next 20 minutes, gently descending to a PASS. where you come upon a large smelly LIVE-STOCK SHED on your left (**3h**). Continue along the track, soon ignoring another track on the right (marked as waypoint ❹ *of Walk 8* on the map; Walk 8 has ascended this track from Palies Sinies). You soon arrive at an small open-sided SHELTER with picnic table (waypoint ❼ *of Walk 6*), from where you can admire the fantastic views both north and south. Now use the notes for Walk 6 on page 60 from the 3h-point, to reach **Ano Perithia** (❶; **3h55min**).

Leaving Ano Perithia, take the road at the left of the rose-coloured CHURCH AND BELL TOWER. Tall, yellow-flowering stems of mullein line the road-side. Follow this road all the way to **Loutses** (**4h35min**), which appears before a stunning

Walk 10: CIRCUIT FROM NIMFES VIA TWO MONIS

Map on reverse of touring map; see photograph on page 19
Distance/time: 12.4km/7.7mi; 3h40min

Grade: ● moderate, with a steep descent to the valley floor below Moni Pantokrator (extra care needed when wet), followed by an ascent to Ag Triada; easy road-walking beyond Klimatia. Overall ups and downs of 500m/1640ft. Some fluorescent dot waymarks, some blue ones.

Important note: At times the stream below Moni Pantokrator will be too full to cross, and you will have to retrace your steps to Nimfes to continue the walk.

Equipment: walking boots or stout shoes, sunhat, sunglasses, suncream, long-sleeved shirt, long trousers, raingear, picnic, water

Picnic suggestion: shady, peaceful Moni Pantokrator

Access: 🚗 to/from Nimfes: park in the wide street near the fountain and public garden (39° 45.355'N, 19° 47.231'E)

Short walk for motorists:
Moni Pantokrator of Nimfes.
3.5km/2.2mi; 55min. ● Easy; stout shoes will suffice. But note that the descent below Moni Pantokrator is steep and can be slippery. Access as main walk.

Follow the main walk until it turns off to Ag Triada (**❸**; 45min). Keep right, to return to Nimfes for your car (55min).

Alternative walk for bus users
Distance/time: 15km/9.3mi; 4h15min

Grade/Equipment/Picnic as main walk for motorists

Access: Roda 🚌 to the Nimfes turn-off about 2km beyond Ag Douli; journey time 50min. Return on 🚌 from Klimatia (*not in the timetables; departs Mon-Fri at 15.00 only*). Walk into **Nimfes** and pick up the main walk at the 'square' (**〇**). Follow it to **Agia Triada** (**❺**; 3h25min), then descend to the bus stop where you meet the road in Klimatia (**❻**; 4h15min).

Shorter walk for bus users:
Nimfes — Moni Ag Triada — Klimatia. 10km/6.2mi; 3h10min. ● Moderate, with a steepish climb of about 275m/ 900ft to the monastery. Transport as main walk. From the FOUNTAIN in Nimfes, cross the road and take the wide road on the right-hand side of the 'SQUARE' (**〇**). A little over five minutes along, you join the main walk at the 45min-point. Pick up the notes at (**❸**) and follow the *Alternative for bus users* above.

This walk calls at two of the island's little-visited *monis*, each in a different setting. Moni Pantokrator of Nimfes sits concealed in a hillside cypress wood, high above a lush valley. Moni Ag Triada adorns a cone-shaped hill with a wonderful view across the olive-studded north. You head from a luxuriant valley full of gardens and trees up to the drier, stonier, olive-clad slopes. Climbing to the summit of a rocky peak, you're surrounded by soft pink heather and shiny-leafed strawberry trees. Nimfes is a kind combination of new and old, sprawling across a ridge. It boasts a nine-spout fountain but — better — after a wet period, an amazingly impressive (for Corfu) waterfall.

73

Start the walk facing Nimfes 'SQUARE' (⦿), with your back to the NINE-SPOUTED FOUNTAIN: take the road at the left of this public garden. Two minutes up, at the top of a rise, fork right on another road through olive groves, to soon come to a CHAPEL AND CEMETERY. Take the path to the right of the chapel down to abandoned **Moni Pantokrator of Nimfes** (❶; **20min**), the peaceful picnic setting shown on page 19.

Go down the steps leading out of the grounds; you come to a SPRING in a minute. Above it is a tiny CAVE CHAPEL where the original hermit lived. Descending into the valley, the clear path, marked with FLUORESCENT DOTS, first curves to the right, then drops to the left. Reaching the flat along the stream, you cross a track, and then the way swings right to cross the stream. *(The log bridge at the crossing point is often swept away, and if the stream is in spate, you may have to retrace your steps to Nimfes to continue the walk — although most readers are finding crossing points upstream or down!)*

If you *can* cross, rise to the FARM TRACK (❷) on the far side and turn right. About 15 minutes along the track, at a junction, keep right. Ignore two turn-offs to the left, cross a concrete bridge, and pass a concrete block shed on the right.

Coming out on the NIMFES ROAD (❸; **45min**), head left for Agia Triada. *(Here the Short walk for motorists turns right, back to Nimfes, and the Alternative walk for bus users joins the main walk.)* Almost at once, pass the football pitch and continue ahead, ignoring the concrete track rising to the right. The valley continues on towards the bulky mass of Pantokrator. Some five minutes along, the way forks. We will go right here, but first — *if you are walking in winter or early spring, when they will be flowing* — make a detour of under 2km return to the steep path down left to the Nimfes WATERFALLS (❹) — seeing is believing!

Then return to the fork and go *sharp left*, climbing the slope. Another steep ascent lies before you, up a rough gravel track. The hillside below is an arboretum. A tiny spring sits on the right some minutes uphill; across the way there's a water catchment tank. Stay on this main track. Ignore tracks joining from either side and keep going until, around 50 minutes uphill, you meet a T-junction where you turn sharp right. From here the chapel is visible on the summit.

The track passes through olive groves and shortly emerges into hillside scrub. Ahead you will see a raw track scarring the hillside below the chapel. Follow this track uphill as it winds its way around the shoulder of the hill, crowned by **Moni Ag Triada** (**2h40min**). From this perch you can enjoy 360° views. Near the chapel there are seats for a relaxing break or perhaps a picnic. By a wooden cross about 100m from the chapel entrance, there are even finer views to the north.

Leaving, retrace your steps. After about 550m go straight on (right) at the T-junction. The blue-waymarked trail now follows an old mule track into the upper part of Nimfes. Turn right, back to the 'SQUARE' and your car (⦿; **3h40min**).

Walk 11: CIRCUIT FROM SOKRAKI

See map on the reverse of
touring map
Circuit for motorists
Distance/time: 5.4km/3.4mi;
2h20min
Grade: ● easy walking on roads
and tracks, with just one short
stretch on paths; ascents of about
180m/600ft overall; partly Corfu
Trail waymarked
Equipment: stout shoes with
ankle support, sunhat,
sunglasses, suncream, long-
sleeved shirt, long trousers,
picnic, water, fleece, raingear
Picnic: anywhere en route
Access: 🚌 to Sokraki; motorists
park by the side of the main road
as you leave Sokraki for Zigos
(39° 43.025'N, 19° 47.880'E).
**Alternative walks for bus
users** (notes on pages 76-77)
**1 Troumpeta to Spartilas or
Pyrgi via Sokraki.** 11.3km/7mi;
2h55min. ● Easy walking on
roads and tracks, with just one
short stretch on paths; initial
ascent of 175m/560ft on a road,
in full sun. Equipment/Picnic as

above, but take swimwear if
going on to Pyrgi. Access by
🚌 (Roda or Sidari bus) to
Troumpeta; journey time 35min.
Return on 🚌 from Spartilas
(journey time 40min) or Pyrgi/
Ipsos (journey time 25min)
2 Troumpeta to Sokraki.
5.8km/3.6mi; 1h15min. ●
Grade/Equipment/Picnic/Access
as Alternative walk 1 above.
Return on 🚌 from Sokraki.
Follow Alternative walk 1 along
the road to **Sokraki** (**○**). Only
one return bus, at 15.30 (Mon-
Sat only); journey time 1h25min
3 Sokraki to Spartilas or Pyrgi.
5.3km/3.3mi; 1h45min. ● Easy
walking on roads and tracks;
minimal ascent. Equipment/
Picnic as above, but take swimwear if going on to Pyrgi. Access
by 🚌 to Sokraki (only one a
day, at 14.00, Mon-Fri only).
Follow Alternative walk 1 from
Sokraki (**○**; the 1h10min-
point); return by bus as Alternative walk 1. Corfu Trail
waymarking. *Highly recommended*

T his walk, following the Corfu Trail for part of the way,
runs along the spine of an abrupt escarpment wall
stretching from east to west, severing the head of the island.
The views are fine, stretching both northward and to the
south — from subdued rolling countryside to a bright,
curvaceous coastline. This is rural Corfu at its best.

Start the walk from the parking
place east of **Sokraki** (**○**), on a
bend just outside the village, by a
SHRINE some metres past the
'Sokraki' sign. You are already on
the Corfu Trail, and your route is
waymarked with a yellow arrow
on pole at the right. Fork right
on the track here, to return to the
crest of the ridge. Within 10
minutes you're above a cascade
of terraced plots running down
the valley floor. A little further

on, the track forks: keep left
(more or less straight ahead; *the
track to the right is your return
route*). Soon the mass of Pantokrator appears (try to ignore the
rubbish tips to the left of the
track). Sgourades is seen across
the valley.
The track descends to a CLEARING.
Fork right to leave the clearing
on a lovely woodland path and
descend to the valley floor.
Minutes from the clearing, you

Alternative walks for bus users

Start off in the hamlet of **Troumpeta** (ⓐ), just at the top of the pass (where the bus stops). Head back southeast along the road towards Corfu Town. Some 50m/yds downhill, fork left on a road climbing the face of the escarpment. This road, which does not see much traffic, will take you all the way to Sokraki. Early on in the climb, you're overlooking the central lowlands and, further east, the noticeable hayfields of the Ropa Plain. Liapades, over to the right, is the first village to appear. Shortly after, Doukades creeps into sight. Some **15min** uphill, the panorama extends to the north. On a clear day you can see the Theapondinisi Islands: Othoni (the largest), Erikoussa (over to the right) and Sanothraki — all inhabited but untouched by tourism, save for one small hotel on Erikoussa. (The islands can be reached daily from Corfu Town by slow ferry or more quickly by ferry from Ag Stefanos in the west.) Continuing towards Sokraki, you pass by orchards, vineyards, and small gardens — all with backdrops of maquis. Cypress trees dot the hillsides. The bold mound of Pantokrator fills the

view. Eventually you round a bend and look across a cultivated basin to Sokraki. Entering the village, you snatch a view of the gulf. Turn left at a T-junction, to walk through the centre of **Sokraki** (**1h10min**), passing a CHURCH on the left. Follow the one-way traffic system, ignoring all turn-offs to the right and coming to a café on the left. (Alternative walk 2 ends here; Alternative walk 3 begins here.)

The ongoing walk to Spartilas now follows part of the Corfu Trail and is waymarked with yellow arrows and dots. You are already on the Trail: follow the road to the eastern edge of the village and, a bit further on, at a Y-FORK (Ⓞ) with a shrine to the left and a pole with a Corfu Trail waymark arrow on the right, pick up the Circuit for motorists on page 75. Follow this to the 1H05MIN-POINT (❷), which you will reach after **2h15min**. The main circuit turns right here, on the track, but you turn *left*. Your two-wheeled track soon becomes a narrow tarmac country lane and takes you to Spartilas, past carefully tended vineyards and a SMALL LAKE full of noisy toads on your left.

pass between terraced fields amidst the scrub. Keep to the main path as it bears right here, but ignore all faint paths off to the right. The path is interrupted by a crossing BULLDOZED TRACK (❶), but continues on the far side — alongside another bulldozed track. Path and track converge at a STONE HUT, then the path continues separately. The clear path bears slightly right, as you descend through

overgrown and abandoned plots, hemmed in by trees and bushes. Some of the terraces you clamber down while following this beautiful, wooded path are quite high.

When you meet the track again, follow it for just 50m/yds, then pick up your path again, on the left. Emerging from the scrub, you come into farmland — olive groves, fruit trees, vegetable plots, and vineyards. The way

Small lake and vineyards on the way to Spartilas

Follow the lane to the hairpin bend of a road, where you turn right. A minute downhill, you have an excellent view of Spartilas from a parking area on the right. **Spartilas (2h55min)** is set in a crease in the mountain wall, with a superb outlook over the gulf. There is an (unmarked) BUS STOP just past the CHURCH (ⓑ) above to the left as you enter the village. *(Alternative walks 1 and 3 end here.)*

But if you still have some bounce left in you, why not walk on to Pyrgi, just over an hour away? It's a pleasant descent if you have a good sense of direction *(no waymarking when last surveyed) and there isn't too much traffic. To get there, walk a bit further into the village, to the pretty yellow café on the right (with flowerpots, seats and post box outside). After a break, turn right downhill along the alley at the right of the café. Then pretty much just follow your nose (knowing where you are heading) or the map — or our GPS track. The route takes you down to a hairpin bend in the road near the sea front in **Pyrgi**, by a BUS STOP to the right (ⓒ; 1h05min from Spartilas). The beach is nearby to the right.

now heads across the right-hand side of the valley. A minute along, you come to a concrete wall below a vineyard, on the far side of which stands a pergola. Swing right in front of the wall, to reach a TRACK just above (❷; **1h05min**).

Turn right on the track *(the Alternative walks turn left)*. After several minutes, at a fork, bear right uphill. Keep on this track, ignoring side-turnings. As you ascend the hillside, the views to the east and south are superb, the islands of Lazaretto and Vidos being clearly visible, as well as Corfu Town, the Halkiopoulos Lagoon and the hills beyond. Keep following the track until it bends sharply round to the right and crosses a small plateau, where you rejoin your outward track. Turn left; in 10 minutes you are back at your car on the edge of **Sokraki** (◉; **2h20min**).

Walk 12: TWO WALKS FROM CAPE DRASTIS

See photographs on pages 1, 22 and cover

Walk a: Peroulades circuit for motorists

Distance/time: 10km/6.2mi; 2h45min

Grade: ● easy-moderate: some stretches are stony, steep and slippery when wet; ups/downs of 200m/650ft overall; little shade; some blue waymarking

Equipment: boots or stout shoes with good ankle support, sunhat, suncream, sunglasses, swimwear, picnic, water

Picnic: at the cove

Access: 🚌 or 🚗 to/from Peroulades; park in the village square (39° 47.292'N, 19° 40.380'E)

Short walk: Cape Drastis. 2.8km/1.8mi; 1h10min. ● Grade/equipment/accesss as main walk. Follow the main walk to the cape; return the same way.

Walk b: Peroulades to Magoulades for bus users

Distance/time: 12km/7.5mi; 3h55min

Grade: ● easy to moderate; overall climbs totalling about 200m/650ft, with one fairly steep ascent of about 80m/260ft, lasting 10 minutes. The track to Cape Drastis may be unpleasantly trafficked in summer.

Equipment: walking boots or shoes with good grip, sunhat, sun-glasses, suncream, long-sleeved shirt, long trousers, fleece, raingear, swimwear, picnic, water

Picnic suggestion: anywhere at the cape

Access: 🚌 to Peroulades; journey time 1h20min. Return on 🚌 from Magoulades; journey time 1h10min

Short walk: see Short walk a

The magnificent bluffs of Cape Drastis will take your breath away. Minuscule off-shore islands, finely etched with circles, look fresh off a potters' wheel. A tiny cove, set deep in the cliff-hanging cape, is a peaceful bathing spot outside high season. (The sandy village beach at the foot of the high cliffs shown on the cover is just as impressive, but usually more crowded.) From the cape Walk a follows the coast as far as the Canal d'Amour, while Walk b heads into the quiet inland hills, under the shade of the ubiquitous olive tree, to the walled-in silence of two monasteries.

Both versions of the walk begin at the PARKING AREA/BUS STOP (**◉**) just below the village square in **Peroulades**. Walk some 30m/yds further into the village along the main road. Then turn right up a concrete lane signposted 'CAPE DRASTIS' (amongst others). Head up to the CHURCH and SCHOOL (in the same grounds), then keep straight uphill, climbing a motorable track past the left-hand side of the school. Keeping to this

main track, cross the brow of the hill and begin descending. In high season you will encounter traffic here, although outside July and August there should only be a trickle. Albania, stretching across the horizon in front of you, is a continuous line of mountains.

Some 50m/yds downhill, climb up left to a viewpoint, but be very *careful* here: without warning, you'll find yourself on the edge of a precipice, where dazzling, pearl-white cliffs slice their way around the point. Past the viewpoint, ignore the track heading inland; keep straight on. The VIEW *par excellence* (**❶**) over this beauty spot, shown on page 1, unfolds three minutes later. You look out over an arc of islets just off-shore. The tiny COVE at **Cape Drastis** (**❷**; **30min**) is an excellent swimming spot, as it is not too deep and it's easy to scramble out of the water. The backdrop is an impressive white wall rising straight up out of a crystal-blue sea. In high season there are likely to be fellows here renting umbrellas and sunbeds and selling cold drinks. *(From here the Short walk and Walk b retrace steps to Peroulades.)*

Walk a retraces steps from the cove for only 200m; then, instead of following the hairpin bend to the right, we go straight ahead on another track. It curves left initially, then bends right. Some 600m after joining this track, be sure to turn *sharp* left uphill (**❸**; blue waymark). Rising at first, the track then descends towards the coast. Beyond some AERIALS (and more fabulous views), *keep to this coastal track* when the blue-waymarked route heads inland 100m past the aerials. After about 1km (now on a farm track), you come to a T-junction on the edge of Sidari. Turn right for 130m, to a road. Follow this to the left past restaurants galore; then, as the main road swings right, keep straight ahead to the **Canal d'Amour** (**❹**; **1h35min**; see page 21).

Return to the road go straight ahead. Pass the lane that you took from the coast and after another 650m (just past a travel agency and the next, three-storey house on the right), turn right on a grassy track (a blue waymark is on a pole opposite). After 100m, turn left on a lane, pass a house on the right, and continue westwards for 1.5km to a T-junction with your outward route, not far west of the aerials. Retrace your steps to the junction where you originally turned sharp left (**❸**) and now go straight ahead, rejoining your track from Peroulades not far south of the 'viewpoint *par excellence*'. Retrace your steps to your car at **Peroulades** (**O**; **2h45min**).

Walk b now turns right below the school, along the village road. Three minutes along, take the first tarred lane branching off to the right, signposted 'BEACH'. Keep left at the first junction for 'BEACH', but turn right at the next junction on a wide road signed 'TO THE BEACH'. After 200m you come to a parking area on the clifftop. Just below you (but still out of sight) stretches the spectacular beach shown on page 22 and the cover. Only a collar of sand separates the sea from the base of the high cliffs. A steep walkway plonks you down onto **Logas Beach** (**❸**) in two minutes.

Return from the beach to the turn-off and head right towards Avliotes, following a winding country road between fields. At the junction, a good five minutes along, fork right (to continue more or less straight ahead). Some 25 minutes from the beach, meet the main road and head uphill to the right, through **Avliotes** (**1h40min**). A good five minutes sees you at the far end of this unprepossessing

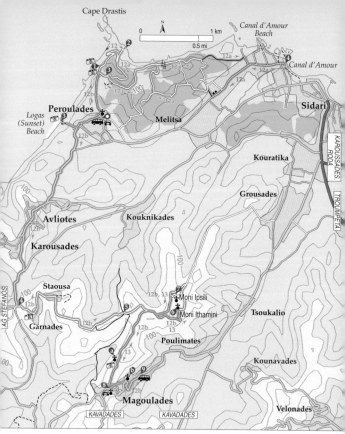

village where, at a junction, you head left towards Ag Stefanos (signposted).

About eight minutes later, ignore the wide AVLIOTES BYPASS ROAD to the left, but take the *next* left turn, an unsigned lane (**4**). The road climbs towards Garnades. After a steep uphill section, ignore the turning to the right and continue ahead. *Zorro* — masked sheep with uneven black socks — sometimes graze the inclines here. When the tarred road ends, at a pink house, continue on a track striking uphill to the right. Shortly, Cape Arilla and Gravia Island appear through an open 'V' in the hills to your right. Keep straight ahead along the track. Soon you have views to the left to Avliotes,

a blend of pinkish buildings stepping the crest of a ridge on the far side of the valley. It looks more attractive when seen from afar.

Half an hour up from the road junction where you turned left for Garnades you reach a FIVE-WAY JUNCTION of tracks (**5**). Pick up the notes now for Walk 13 from the 30MIN-POINT to visit the two monasteries (**6** and **7**) and descend to the small CHURCH (**8**) at the upper end of **Magoulades**.

From here take the downhill road opposite this church to descend through the village. Less than 20 minutes downhill come to the BUS SHELTER (**9**; **3h55min**) for buses to Corfu Town.

Walk 13: MONI ITHAMINI AND MONI IPSILI

See map opposite (waypoints are shared with Walk 12)
Distance/time: 5km/3mi; 1h20min
Grade: ● easy; stout shoes will suffice; minimal ups and downs

Picnic: at one of the *monis*
Access: 🚌 to/from Magoulades (bus times are inconvenient); park near the small church at the top of the village (39° 45.363'N, 19° 40.472'E)

An ideal leg stretcher, a visit to these two monasteries is a peaceful change from the busy Cape Drastis corner of the island. Moni Ipsili is one of the largest and wealthiest monasteries on Corfu, founded early in the 10th century. Before heading home, *do* visit the splendid main church of Ag Theodori in (lower) Magoulades as well.

Start the walk in colourful **Magoulades** by following the road diagonally opposite the small CHURCH (**8**), walking all the way along the top of the ridge. In **30min** you join a track coming from the left, and in less than a minute you are at the junction for the two monasteries. Take the tarmac drive off right down to **Moni Ithamini** (**6**; under **35min**), snuggled into a hillside hollow under citrus trees, loquats and elms. This monastery now houses a European Youth Centre.

From Moni Ithamini take the path around the left of the building, then follow a track uphill, round the shoulder of the hill. The next monastery is hidden among the trees above you on the left. Turn left at the next junction and follow a concrete lane up to **Moni Ipsili** (**7**; **40min**); its valuable icons and paintings are unfortunately kept locked away.

To continue the walk, descend the concrete lane back to the road and follow it to the left, retracing your outward route. If you didn't detour earlier to the ISOLATED CHURCH (**1**) up on your right some 10 minutes along, perhaps do so now — there are some good views to enjoy. The road brings you back to your car by the small CHURCH in **Magoulades** (**8**; **1h20min**).

Moni Ipsili

Walk 14: THREE WALKS TO CAPE ARILLA

See also photograph on pages 10-11

Distance/time, Grade, Access, etc: see Walks a-c below

Picnic suggestions for Walks a and b: see notes beside the photograph on pages 10-11

Walk a: Port Timone from Afionas

Distance/time: 2.3km/1.4mi; 1h10min (3.2km/1h50min with detour to cave chapel)

Grade: ● moderate descent/ascent of 100m/330ft

Equipment: stout shoes, sunhat, picnic, water

Access: 🚌 to/from Afionas; park in the village, at the end of the road, keeping well clear of the square where the bus turns round (39° 43.364'N, 19° 39.623'E).

Walk b: Cape Arilla from Afionas

Distance/time: 1km/0.7mi; 30min

Grade: ● easy; wear stout shoes

Access: as Walk a above

Walk c: Port Timone from Ag Georgios

Distance/time: 8km/5mi; 2h 40min (3h20min with detour)

Grade: ● moderate, with overall descents/ascents of 400m/1300ft

Equipment: walking boots or stout shoes with good grip and ankle support, sunhat, sunglasses, suncream, long-sleeved shirt, fleece, long trousers, rainwear, swimwear, picnic, water

Picnic suggestion: Ag Georgios

Access: 🚌 to/from Ag Georgios beach (39° 43.007'N, 19° 40.819'E)

Three walks for those of you who want to enjoy Corfu's northwest coast without expending the energy needed for Walk 15. The most attractive hilltop 'garden' village of Afionas will give you splendid views and good opportunities to stretch your legs — while the short hike from Ag Georgios is more demanding, but lets you relax afterwards on a gorgeous stretch of beach.

Walk a starts at the SQUARE in Afionas. Make for Cape Arilla: standing with your back to the CHURCH (❶), head off into the alley 10m/yds to the left (by the sign for the PORTO TIMONE restaurant. After 70m/yds, turn left on a path. After 600m/yds, take the path forking right (❷; with a fence on the right). This path, though not always immediately obvious, is well defined. The views over the inviting headland and bay are most appealing. The crystal-clear sea is almost hypnotic. This short path leads to a fine VIEWPOINT (❸) overlooking the twin coves at Port Timone; rounding the hillside, these two bright little

coves, shown on pages 10-11, shine up at you — a perfect picnic setting. Return the same way and walk down to the coves. In ancient times the larger one was known as the 'Tiller's Port' (**Port Timone**; (❹; 30min), where boats came to shelter from approaching storms. A collar of land separates the two. The promontory joined to this tiny necklace of land is tightly woven in maquis. Three trails with colour-coded signposts lead off from the viewpoint — one of them to the hermit's cave chapel on the hillside 20 minutes away, which you might like to visit. Return the same way to **Afionas** (❶; 1h10min).

Walk b climbs the wide alley shown above (signed to 'SUNSET 200M', opposite the CHURCH in **Afionas** (**❶**). This leads past a restaurant to seats at a VIEW-POINT (**4min**) — a lovely picnic spot. See the notes in the photograph caption on page 11 to guide you to the next view-point (**❸; 14min**). Return the same way to **Afionas** (**30min**).
Walk c heads from the south end of **Ag Georgios Beach** (**◯**) to the north end, from where you follow the road that ascends to Afionas. A steep 15-minute climb up the road takes you to a T-junction, where you turn left. Ten minutes later you're in the square at **Afionas** (**❶; 25min**). Now complete WALK A above, before returning to **Ag Georgios** the same way (**2h40min**).

The lovely village of Afionas (top) and the Cape Arilla coastline

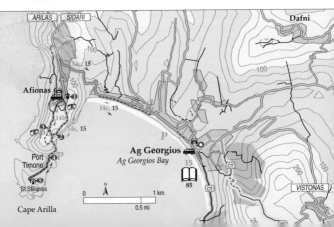

Walk 15: FROM PALEOKASTRITSA TO CAPE ARILLA

Paleokastritsa • Lakones • Makrades • Ag Georgios • Afionas

Map continues on page 83; see also photographs on pages 10-11, 12-13, 83
Distance/time: 15km/9.3mi; 4h55min
Grade: ● strenuous, with overall ascents/descents of 500m/1650ft. The paths are slippery when wet.
Equipment: walking boots or stout shoes with good grip and ankle support, sun -hat, -glasses, -cream, long-sleeved shirt, fleece, long trousers, rainwear, swimwear, picnic, water
Picnic suggestion: Ag Georgios, Cape Arilla (see Walk 14)
Access: 🚌 to the Paleokastritsa terminus (journey time 40min). Return on 🚌 from Afionas; journey time 2h15min. Or telephone from a café at Afionas for a Sidari taxi, to take you to Sidari, for better bus connections.

Paleokastritsa is Corfu's tourist mecca. But, fortunately, tourist development has not yet disfigured this natural asset. This walk is all about wonderful views. After the initial steep climb up to the hill village of Lakones, your first views are back down to the pine-fringed beaches around Paleokastritsa. Still climbing, the walk heads inland to the attractive village of Makrades and, soon afterwards, as you descend an old zigzag mule trail, there are more glorious views over the shimmering horseshoe bay of Ag Georgios. After a longish stretch along the sandy beach, the path again climbs to the hilltop village of Afionas, with the final part of the walk (an 'out and back route') providing yet more fine views over the twin coves of Port Timone.

The walk begins at the CAR PARK/BUS TERMINUS (●) in **Paleokastritsa**. Walk back along the main road for about 200m/yds. Then take the first turn-off left, just beyond another parking area and opposite the SUPERMARKET KATHY. Some 70m/yds uphill, go right at a fork. This is where the real ascent begins. Continue up this road for about 10 minutes (just under 400m/yds), to a point where the road flattens out. Turn left here on a track. Soon the track forks; keep right here (signposted). After about 100m/yds you're on a lovely old stone-paved path. A few minutes up, a path joins from the right; keep straight on, under the shade of olive trees. Half-moons of terracing stretch

84

across the hillside. Midway up to Lakones, you enter a passageway slicing up through a vertical rock face. Out of the passage and back into terraced hillsides, you cross a track, and then enter **Lakones** (**❶**). The path veers right, to where an alley cuts across in front of you. Turn left up the alley and, on meeting the ROAD (**40min**), turn left. *(Walk 16 turns right here.)*
At the end of the built-up area you come to a FIRST SET OF TRAFFIC LIGHTS (**❷**) controlling one-way traffic along a narrow stretch of road. Under 100m/yds *before* the second set of traffic lights, you come to an isolated parade of low buildings on the left. Leave the road here, taking

steps up to a path (opposite the last building, a woodcarver's emporium: a sign on the roof and the far side of the house reads 'ALKI'S ARTIST OLIVE WOOD PRODUCTION').

A little over 10 minutes up the path, a STEEL FRAME (the remains of a greenhouse) is visible across the valley floor on the left. Ignoring any side paths to the right or left, keep to the main path (although it may be narrow and edged with prickly plants at first). When you are directly across the valley from the framework, continue along the main path: it widens out and after about 100m/yds bends left,

rounds the head of the shallow valley and comes to a T-junction, where you turn right. Quickly reaching the MAIN ROAD, turn left (**1h05min**).

Follow the road to the outskirts of Vistonas. Just past the **Vistonas** sign, you can take a SHORT-CUT (**❸**): bear left on a concrete lane (beside a SHRINE at the side of the road). It takes you to the CEMETERY CHURCH. Walk to the right of the church on a narrow downhill path through olive trees, rejoining the road after 200m/yds. Follow it to the left, to the MAKRADES JUNCTION (**❹; 1h25min**). Now make a dash to the right, before the stall-

Below: the old mule trail down to Ag Georgios Beach

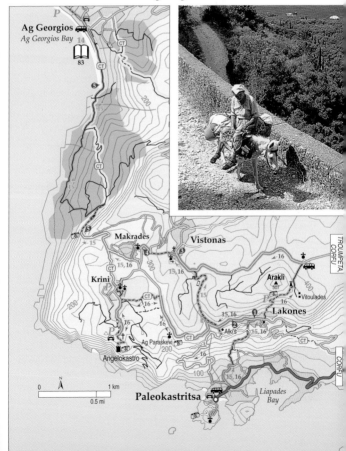

Alley in Lakones and (right) cemetery church at Vistonas (Walk 16)

keepers rush out to insist you taste their local wines from the barrel!

Continue through **Makrades** until, just past the last houses and a cafeneion, you come to a lane cutting across in front of you (concrete to the right and tarmac to the left). Head right along the concrete lane. A few minutes down, a neat concreted track, bordered by low stone walls, joins the track from the left. *(This is where Walk 16 turns left to Krini, another pretty hilltop village.)*

Ten minutes downhill, the track comes to a dead end at a BARRIER for vehicles. Ahead lies the most unexpected sight: a path — the OLD MULE 'ROAD' (**5**) down to the sea — cuts through a corridor in the hillside rock. Once through it, you're virtually 'hanging' out over glorious Ag Georgios Bay; the piercing blue sea, trimmed in turquoise, shimmers below. Clinging to the escarpment, this old mule road descends in zigzags, with views across the translucent bay to Cape Arilla and the Theapondinisi Islands. Ten minutes down, when you join a gravel track, turn left downhill, towards the coast. At the junction that

86

follows, bear right along a track running parallel with the bay. This is a beautiful stroll, looking through the olive trees down onto the green sea. Various tracks lead down to the sea; you could explore any of them. About 50 minutes after leaving the zigzag mule path, you reach **Ag Georgios Beach** (**6**; **2h50min**). The RESORT of **Ag Georgios** is not based around a village, but has grown up as a result of the popularity of this 2km-long sandy beach. The resort is divided into three sections because there is no coastal road all along the seafront. Having perhaps stopped for a swim or refreshment, pick up the notes for WALK 14C now (page 83), first climbing to **Afionas** (**7**; **3h45min**). Its strategic setting makes Afionas prone to winds, but the villagers must think the views compensate for the inconvenience. From the square make for Cape Arilla by following the notes for WALK 14A on page 82 *(and note that the waypoint numbering differs on the two walks)*. You should be back at the SQUARE in **Afionas** in **4h55min**.

Walk 16: GRAND CIRCUIT FROM PALEOKASTRITSA

Paleokastritsa • Lakones • Mt Arakli • Makrades • Krini •
Angelokastro • Paleokastritsa

See photographs on pages 12-13, 25, 26 and opposite

Distance/time: 13km/8mi; 4h

Grade: ●● moderate-strenuous, with an initial ascent of 450m/1500ft and a descent of 300m/1000ft at the end. Some of the paths can be slippery when wet; possibility of vertigo at Angelokastro

Equipment: walking boots, sunhat, suncream, sunglasses, long-sleeved shirt, raingear, picnic, water

Picnic suggestions: Mt Arakli, Krini threshing floor, Angelokastro

Access: 🚌 to/from the car park below Paleokastritsa monastery (35° 9.655'N, 25° 38.907'E). Or 🚐 (journey time 40min)

Shorter walks (access and equipment as main walk)

1 Mt Arakli obelisk. 5km/3mi; 2h30min. ● Moderate-strenuous, with an overall ascent/descent of 450m/1500ft. Follow the main walk as far as the OBELISK (❷) on the east flank of **Mt Arakli** (1h 20min); return the same way.

2 Lakones. 2.5km/1.5mi; 1h30min. ● Moderate, with an overall ascent/descent of 275m/900ft (the ascent to Lakones is steep). Follow the main walk up to **Lakones** and, when you reach the main road in the village, turn left to ALKI'S OLIVE WOOD shop (see the last paragraph on page 84 to identify this). Turn down the steps at the far side of this

shop and follow the main walk from the 3h15-point back down to Paleokastritsa.

3 Angelokastro. 7.8km/4.9mi; 3h10min. ●● Moderate-strenuous, with an overall ascent/descent of 330m/1075ft (the ascents to Lakones and the castle are steep). A very popular route with 'Landscapers'! Follow the main walk up to **Lakones** (❶) and from there walk along the road through the village towards Krini, passing Bella Vista ('the best view in Europe'), a couple of restaurants with tables overlooking the turquoise coastline, and a convent. Some 450m/yds past the convent, on a long stretch of straight road, take a path on the left indicated by a yellow CORFU TRAIL MARKER on a pole. This descends into an olive grove and stream bed. After a few metres, leave the stream bed by taking a path to the right. Bear right and follow the path ahead, through the trees. It soon becomes a track and climbs. On a bend, take a path (by a rock), climbing gently to the main village road on the edge of Krini. Turn left here and follow the road downhill for 10 minutes, to **Angelokastro** (❻). On the return leg, you could divert into **Krini** (❺) or visit the old threshing floor just outside the village (see the **P** symbol on the map) before heading back to **Paleokastritsa**.

It's hard to imagine Paleokastritsa as a humble fishing village before the onset of tourism. Set amid a sequence of turquoise bays and rocky coves, backed by tumbling green hillsides and the dominant bulk of Mt Arakli, it must have been incomparably beautiful. While tourist development has taken a definite toll, the natural beauty of the

87

landscape can perhaps be best appreciated by venturing into the mountainous hinterland, with many viewpoints over the dramatic coastline. This walk makes a circuit up the flanks of Mt Arakli, giving unsurpassed views of the Bay of Liapades. It follows old stone-paved paths and donkey tracks, visiting three attractive hillside villages on the way and then, returning towards the coast, it leads you to a steep climb up to the rocky fortress of Angelokastro. The few skeletal remains have little to offer, but its sheer-sided perch will leave you in awe — if not fright — as you peer down into a milky-green sea 330m/1075ft below.

Begin the walk by following the notes for WALK 15 on page 84. When you reach the main road in **Lakones** (**❶**; **40min**), turn right. Walk along the narrow street for 200m/yds, watching out for traffic, then climb steps up to the left (just past a BUTCHER'S SHOP). In half a minute, where the alley bears right, keep climbing the steps, ignoring all side-alleys. In two minutes, at a T-junction at the top of the village, turn right uphill. This path, which is partly cobbled and with shallow steps, ascends up the SLOPES OF **Mt Arakli**. Follow the cobbled path away from the village, out onto the open hillside, with views down to the coast — a splendid place to picnic.

After some zigzags the path levels out and soon turns inland. In 20 minutes you reach a stony track with a white OBELISK on your left (**❷**; **1h10min**). This is the highest point on the walk, with Mt Arakli on the left. Turn left along the track and follow it downhill to the DOUKADES/VISTONAS ROAD (**1h15min**). There is a BUS SHELTER on the right, and an isolated church on a small hillside opposite is a prominent landmark.

Turn left and follow the road for 25 minutes, to the outskirts of Vistonas. As you near the village, you join WALK 15 again and can take a short-cut by following a concrete lane to the left: it starts just past the **Vistonas** sign, beside a SHRINE (**❸**) at the side of the road and passes a CHURCH on the left. From the church keep straight downhill on a path through olive trees, rejoining the road after 200m/yds. Approaching the MAKRADES JUNCTION (**❹**; **2h10min**), make a dash to the right, before the stall-keepers

rush out to tempt you with their offers!

Continue through **Makrades** until, just past the last houses and a *cafeneion*, you come to a lane cutting across in front of you (concrete to the right and tarmac to the left). Head right along the concrete lane; the concrete soon turns to gravel. A few minutes down, a concrete lane joins the track from the left. Turn left on this lane. *(Walk 15 continues to the right here, down the track.)* Follow the lane through olive trees, then garden plots and vineyards, before climbing up to **Krini** (**❺**; **2h20min**). Entering the village, you reach a T-junction with a narrow alley. You will turn left here, but first you could make a short diversion to a lovely picnic setting: turn *right* and follow the alley for two minutes, to reach the beautiful stone-laid threshing floor shown on page 26; it's just outside the village. In spring this site is a mass of wild flowers, and there are seats from which you can contemplate the views north along the western coastline. When you are ready to continue, return along the alley into the village 'centre' — a 'square' — with a small tree in the middle. Turn right here, following the alley to the outskirts of the village. Then continue straight on down the hill towards Angelokastro.

Ten minutes downhill you're at the foot of a stumpy tower of scrub-covered rock, crowned by the (extensively renovated) castle ruins. Take the path leading off the parking area, and follow it to the top, keeping right at the fork three minutes up. From **Angelo-kastro** the views are superb. You look along the escarpment wall as it slides off into a bay indented with sandy coves. On a clear day you can see across the island to Corfu Town — hence the strategic importance of this medieval fortress. (But for shade, I like to picnic in the olive groves on the hill opposite the castle, reached by a path from the car park.)

On the return to Krini, you can use paths to cut out some bends in the road. When you reach the top of the hill, on the village outskirts (beside the wall of the first house on the right), turn right, down into an olive grove. There is a Corfu Trail marker on a telegraph pole at the right. Follow this delightful path, gently descending, and when you meet a track in four minutes, turn left. One minute later, when the track ends, keep straight ahead along the path. In another four minutes descend into a dry stream bed. Turn left along the stream bed and, after a few metres, follow the path up to the right, out of the gully and onto the LAKONES ROAD (**3h**).

Turn right along the road. Some 15 minutes along (about five minutes past Taverna Bellavista — 'the best view in Europe'), you're back at ALKI'S OLIVE WOOD SHOP; **3h15min**). Descend steps alongside the building. Follow this sometimes overgrown path down to a concreted track. Continue down the track for some 40 minutes, all the way back to **Paleokastritsa**. There is a BUS STOP is a couple of minutes along to the right — or return to the CAR PARK/BUS TERMINUS (**○**; **4h**) at the foot of the monastery hill.

Walk 17: THREE BEACHES

Distance/time, Grade: see individual walks. *Note also some alternative tracks on the map.*

Access/equipment: as Walk 19 overleaf (trainers will suffice, and take sorkelling gear, plenty of water and sun protection)

Picnic suggestions: the beaches

Walk a: Rovina and Limni
Distance/time: 7.3km/4.5mi; 2h30min
Grade: ● easy to Rovina, with minimal ups and downs; a bit more taxing to Limni, with ascents/descents of 150m/000ft

Walk b: Liniodoros
Distance/time: 12km/7.5mi; 3h40min
Grade: ● quite strenuous; ups and downs of 240m/800ft

These walks explore the headlands and coves south of Paleokastritsa. As you would expect, you'll find plenty of company at nearby Rovina, but pebbly Liniodoros and the double beach of Limni (shown below) are quieter.

Walk a: Follow Walk 19 overleaf as far as the fork just past Villa Birlis (**1**). Turn right here: yellow arrows indicate the way down to **Rovina Beach** (**a**; **40min**). Retrace steps to the junction (**1**) and keep ahead to a tarred lane (**2**). Turn sharp right. This becomes concreted and passes a (gated) turn-off right to a spectacular view over your goal. Finally a path takes you down to **Limni Beach** (**b**; **1h20min**). Retrace steps to **Paleokastritsa** CAMPING (**O**).

Walk b: Follow Walk 19 overleaf to the 50min-point (**3**), then turn right on a track. After 40m, at a fork, go left. Keep to this track all the way to isolated little **Liniodoros Cove** on **Cape Ag Iliodoros** (**c**; **1h35min**), with fine views across Liapades Bay. Retrace steps to **Paleokastritsa** CAMPING (**O**; **3h40min**).

Walk 18: MARMARO HILLS CIRCUIT

Distance/time: 12km/7.4mi; 3h40min

Grade: ● easy-moderate, with graduals ascents of 300m/1000ft

Equipment: stout shoes with good grip or walking trainers, sunhat, sunglasses, suncream, long-sleeved shirt, long trousers, raingear, picnic, water

Picnic suggestion: in the hills

Access: 🚌 (journey 35min) or 🚗 to/from Paleokastritsa Camping (39° 40.581'N, 19° 43.521'E)

Walking through beautiful olive groves, circle the Marmaro Hills, terraced in tired stone walls. Then spend some time wandering the alleys of Liapades, a charming, authentic village with old manorial homes and the lovely church of Ag Anastasia.

Start out by following WALK 19 overleaf to the centre of **Liapades** (**40min**) and then on to the **55min**-point (**4**), by a SHRINE in a small upright concrete box.

Head right here, keeping to the CORFU TRAIL. Stay on this main route, ignoring offshoots, until you meet a T-junction (1h35min). Turn left on this track. After 250m/yds the track describes a hairpin bend to the left; 150m/yds further on a track to the right leads to a TV mast, but you turn 90° left. Once more ignore offshoots. At the end of this track (a CONCRETE BLOCK BUILDING is on the right; **5**), turn right and then immediately left.

From this point occasional red arrows confirm that you are on the correct route. After some 15 minutes (just over 1km), ignore a crossing track. Keep left at both of the next junctions (after 500m and 450m further on). You have good views of the escarpment wall cutting across the north of the island. Keep right at the next junction (after 350m). Finally, when a TRACK WITH A LARGE WATER PIPE (**6**) alongside it cuts across in front of you, turn hard left downhill to Liapades. On entering the village, continue

to the right, down a lane. When you meet a narrow road, follow it a short way left uphill, then take the first right and, at the end of this alley, descend to the right, to the village square (3h).

To return along your outgoing route, keep left at the bottom of the square. You'll be back at **Paleokastritsa** CAMPING (**O**) after **3h40min**.

Walk 19: FROM PALEOKASTRITSA TO SGOMBOU

Paleokastritsa • Liapades • Ginades • Trivouliattica • Sgombou

See also photograph on pages 11-12
Distance/time: 17km/10.6mi; 5h
Grade: ● moderate, with gradual ascents of about 350m/ 1150ft overall. There is a short, very awkward descent down a cleft near the start of the walk (dangerous if wet); less agile walkers should avoid this by starting out from the Elly Beach Hotel or Liapades.
Equipment: walking boots or stout shoes with good grip, sun-hat, sunglasses, suncream, long-sleeved shirt, long trousers, rain-gear, swimwear, picnic, water

Picnic suggestion: Gavrolimni
Access: 🚌 (journey 35min) or 🚗 to Paleokastritsa Camping (39° 40.581'N, 19° 43.521'E). Return on 🚌 from Sgombou (Paleokastritsa bus), to Corfu Town (journey time 20min), or back to Paleokastritsa Camping for your car
Shorter walk: Paleokastritsa — Liapades — Gianades. 8.5km/ 5.3mi; 2h20min; ● easy if you start at Elly Beach Hotel; equipment, access *by bus* as main walk; return by 🚌 from Gianades (Mon-Fri only). Follow the main walk to Gianades.

Meander through mossy olive groves to the sound of chirping birds and, if you're unlucky, the blast of a shotgun — someone after those chirping birds. Cross a plain squared by ditches and cushioned in grass, with not an olive tree in sight. Plod along an open, shallow valley littered with scrub and trees. In spring, orchids, stars of Bethlehem, anemones and wild geraniums adorn this countryside. In autumn, the dry and faded, rocky hillsides are embellished with cyclamen and *Sternbergia,* the fields carpeted in squill and crocuses. This hike across the Ropa Plain is especially suitable for bus users. Motorists may prefer Walk 20, but there's no reason why drivers couldn't start or end this walk by bus.

The walk starts at **Paleokas-tritsa** CAMPING (○). Head back along the main road towards Corfu Town. Some 80 paces beyond SUPERMARKET ARIS (just past a scooter rental shop), turn right on a concrete lane, part of the CORFU TRAIL. At the end of the lane pick up a path between two houses (signposted to the 'ACAPULCO' swimming pool). A couple of minutes across an olive grove, drop down onto a con-crete lane, where the advertised pool is to your right. Cross the lane and climb some steps on the

left. At the top, continue along the somewhat overgrown path to the right. Three minutes from the lane, you look straight down into a cleft in the ridge. Although only about 2m/6ft deep, it's steep — a very awkward descent. *Care and all fours are required. If at all wet it's dangerous! (You may find an old ladder here — or a rope; don't use either unless you're absolutely sure it will take your weight!)*
A steep descent on a path follows. Soon you overlook a cove set in rock walls. Ignore the

path ascending to the left. The path emerges in the grounds of the ELLY BEACH HOTEL (**20min**). Walk to the left of the hotel and pool, to join a road. Head up the road and, shortly, turn left up steps, following **CORFU TRAIL** signposting through the terrace of the CRICKETER'S TAVERNA and then steps. Rejoining the road, after about 70m/yds climb steps up to the right (just past Villa Birlis). Two minutes up, at a fork (❶), go left. *(Walk 17a goes right here for Rovina Beach.)*
On reaching a ROAD (❷), turn left. *(Walk 17a goes right here for Limni Beach.)* Almost immediately, at a fork, head right and enter **Liapades** (**40min**), with its lovely manorial homes, handsome arched doorways and courtyards. Turn left at the T-junction, going downhill at first, and ignoring any turn-offs until you reach the SQUARE. With the CHURCH on your right, leave the square by heading uphill along the alley ahead (with a sign indicating 'no through road'). Again, ignore all turn-offs

until, two minutes up, you come to a T-junction (just beyond a Venetian manor on the left). Turn left here on a wide concrete path. A good five minutes up from the square, a country road cuts across in front of you; turn right. Two minutes along the road, where a track forks off to the right, keep left on the road (❸; **50min**). *(Walk 17b heads right here.)*
Some five minutes later, at the next fork, by a SHRINE in a small upright concrete box (❹; **55min**), keep left. *(Walk 18 goes right here.)* The way soon reverts from surfaced track to gravel. Within the next 15 minutes (just under 1km along), follow the main track to the left. After 250m, turn right (just 10 metres *before* a Y-fork of tracks). Now follow this main route for just over 1km, ignoring any turn-offs, until you come to a T-junction with a CONCRETE BLOCK BUILDING ahead (❺). Go left here, rejoining the **CORFU TRAIL**.
The Ropa Valley comes into view through a V in the hills.

Ropa Valley vineyard

Flat, herbaceous, and dotted with a few trees, it makes a complete transition in the landscape. Slightly further on, you look straight across the centre of the island. A descent follows, down a shallow side-valley. Some five minutes (450m) from the last junction, join a track before a bend and follow it to the right, heading down into the side-valley. (*Don't* take the fainter track immediately to the right.) In the distance stand the black mounds of Mt Ag Georgios near Vatos (Walk 23) and Ag Deka (Walk 24). Ten minutes along, ignore a faint track off to the left and, five minutes later, at a junction, keep right (but *ignore* the *faint* turn-off right just before this junction). Three minutes later a track joins you from the right. Looking across the valley you can see the church in Gianades.

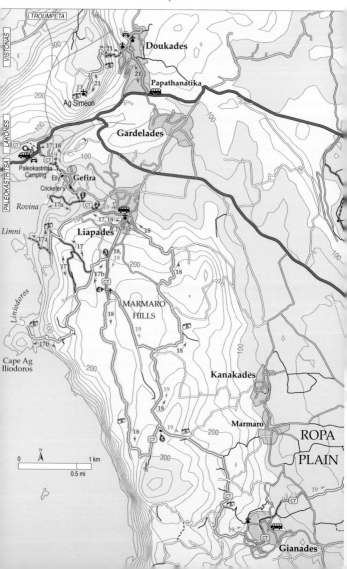

Knowing where you are heading, keep to the Corfu Trail (or use the map) through all the junctions. The Trail avoids the main roads in **Gianades** (**2h20min**) — but also misses the prettiest corner of the village, draped in bougainvillaea, near the CHURCH.

Reaching a T-junction with the KANAKADES ROAD on the far side of Gianades (**2h35min**), turn right. Just 100m/yds along, the ditch which has been on the right-hand side of the road passes under the road and emerges on the left. As soon as you cross this culvert, swing left on a farm track and head across the **Ropa Plain**. Five minutes along, you cross a concrete culvert and a faint track joins you from the right. Keep ahead along the main track, which gradually softens into grass. Ahead and slightly off to your right are several large,

isolated houses. Keep ahead on the grassy track until you meet another grassy track at a T-junction (nearly 20 minutes after leaving the road). There is a WIDE, DEEP DRAINAGE CHANNEL ahead of you (**6**). To continue the walk to Sgombou, you must *leave* the **CORFU TRAIL** now and cross this channel, which may carry water in spring. (If you prefer not to paddle, follow this longer detour route, which adds 30 minutes: turn right here, following the **CORFU TRAIL** south for five minutes, to a country road lined with eucalyptus trees. Leave the **CORFU TRAIL** at this point and turn left on this road for a little over 1km, to the Paleokastritsa road. Turn left again for another 1.2km, to reach the main route at the junction with the GRASS-HOPPER SIGN; **7**)

Out of the drainage channel, cross a lane and keep straight on. When the track fades, make for the line of CYPRESS TREES not far ahead. Closer to the trees, you have to cross another couple of DITCHES. Then veer left, keeping in line with the cypresses. When the trees end, continue straight on in the same direction. Remaining in the grassy field, pick up a path which leads to a faint track, about three minutes from the cypresses. (In spring, when the grass is tall, this track is hardly visible.) Turn right on the track, up to the road (**3h25min**).

Turn right on the road and, after 30m/yds, turn left on a narrow concrete lane with a GRASS-HOPPER SIGN (**7**) at the turning. The concrete gives way to gravel and cuts through a ridge. You

come into a very shallow valley, with an anarchy of vegetation. The escarpment wall reappears, filling the landscape to the north, with Skripero below.

Ten minutes (just under 1km) from the turn-off, ignore a farm track off left (**8**; followed in Walk 20). Three minutes later, where the track goes right to an isolated house, keep left on another track. After 100m/yds bear right along a fainter, earthen track, heading towards a ROW OF PINES. Pass through a gap in a hedge and join a stony track as you reach the pines. Now follow the track. A first pond appears over on your left. **Gavrolimni**, the next pond, follows, almost hidden by the surrounding cultivation. This is a beautiful pastureland setting, with plenty of shade for a picnic break. The track briefly heads between high fences. Ignore two turn-offs to the right a few minutes later. On reaching a road, turn right past VILLA THEA. Keep straight on through the hamlet of **Trivou-liattica** (**4h35min**). Continue north for 25 minutes, to the

On the Ropa Plain

Walk 20: ROPA PLAIN CIRCUIT

Trivouliattica • Ag Noufures • Pelekas • Trivouliattica

Distance/time: 10.5km/6.5mi; 2h55min; 15.5km/9.6mi; 4h05min for bus users

Grade: ● quite easy, with no noticeable ups or downs.

Equipment: trainers or stout shoes with ankle support, sunhat, sunglasses, suncream, long-sleeved shirt, long trousers, raingear, picnic, water

Picnic suggestion: Gavrolimni Pond, Ag Noufures

Access: 🚍 to/from Trivouliat-tica, southwest of Sgombou. Park near Villa Thea, well tucked off the road (39° 39.595'N, 19° 48.489'E). To get there, take the Paleokastritsa road to the crossroads near KM12 and use the walking notes for bus users to reach Trivouliattica. Or 🚐 (Paleokastritsa bus; journey time 20min) to/from Sgombou. Alight from the bus at the stop for the Lucciola Garden, then see walking notes below.

T his is a ramble full of bucolic charm. You pass by ponds, through thickets of tangled foliage, and cross grassy fields. On route you call at Ag Noufures, the charming abandoned monastery shown below. There are no significant ups and downs, so you can just stride out.

Whether on foot from the bus stop or by car, **start off** at the crossroads on the Paleokastritsa road in **Sgombou** — just west of the TRAFFIC LIGHTS and east of the PETROL STATION and the BLUE KM12 SIGN. Head due south on the road past the MARKET (⊙), then turn right immediately, to reach the LUCCIOLA GARDEN, an organic bistro (with rave reviews on Trip Advisor). Continue along the road that passes to the left of this restaurant, towards the cypress trees. Follow the road to the hamlet of **Trivouliattica**. Here another road turns off left, but keep straight on past a set of children's swings, beside more cypress trees. Follow this country lane for 10 minutes, going under

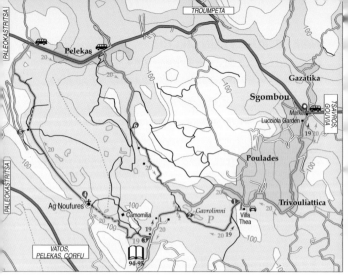

Pelekas
20

Gazatika

Sgombou

Market

Lucciola Garden

TSAVROS, GOUVIA

19

Poulades

6

Trivouliattica

Ag Noufures

Camomilia

Gavrolimni
P

Villa
Thea

VATOS,
PELEKAS, CORFU

19

94-95

an overhead electricity line and passing scattered villas, until you come to VILLA THEA. Motorists should park nearby. If you are on foot from the bus stop, allow 35 minutes to get here.

The **circuit proper starts** on an uphill bend to the right (only 20m/yds past Villa Thea): turn left down a stony track (❶; there is a 3m/9ft-high CONCRETE PILLAR WITH ELECTRICITY METERS on the left at the top of this track). Follow the gently meandering track downhill; after about 10 minutes you pass to the left of **Gavrolimni** POND (❷) where, for a short distance, the track is fenced off on both sides. In winter it's a good-sized pond, frequented by herons and, to a lesser extent, egrets and moorhens. Two large holly oaks at the side of the fenced track mark your approach to this pond. Crossing a broad plain, you'll see another pond over to your right (but in summer it will be dried up). These ponds make a very pleasant picnic setting. Continue along the track until it passes through a line of pretty pines. Some 30m/yds past the

In the grounds of Ag Noufures

pines, bear right on a lesser, faint track which comes to a hedge gap after 100m/yds. Pass through the gap and follow the still-faint track across an open field, to a small house with a red pantiled roof. Join a track at the house and follow it to the left. Off to your left is a small farmstead with a jumble of derelict vehicles behind it. After the track breasts a small rise, there is a fenced-off grove of young olive trees on the hillside to your left.

Just after passing a stone and pantile barn on the right, turn right down a side-track signposted to 'CAMOMILIA' (❸). Continue along this track until it nears Camomilia — a large, secluded country villa with an L-shaped swimming pool. Keep to the left outside the property's boundary fence, to join an indistinct and probably over-grown path. This leads you past another pond, below on your right. Follow this path as it gradually climbs the shoulder of the hill and you reach another pleasant picnic setting (shown on page 97), **Ag Noufures** (❹; **55min**). Inside the churchyard it's cool and fresh.

To continue the walk, stand with the belfry on your left, and head north along the crest, to reach a rough dirt track. Follow it to the right and head back down into the valley. Around 10 minutes from the *moni*, the track forks. Go right (more or less straight on). An old rusty barbed-wire fence runs along the right-hand

side of the track. Minutes later you pass in front of a FARM SHED (❺) where there may be loose dogs. Beyond the shed, continue on an old STONE-LAID TRAIL that goes straight on, ignoring the farm track on the left for the moment. Minutes later, you join this farm track and follow it to the right. Three minutes later, a track joins from the right; keep left here. After a further three minutes, meet a private road and turn right along it. This road takes you in five minutes to the PALEOKASTRITSA ROAD (**1h25min**).

If your legs are sending you messages, you can catch a bus here. To head on, follow the road to the right for 1km — take care, the locals treat it like the Monte Carlo strip! Then turn right uphill on a minor road (just past the BLUE KM14 SIGN). Ignore the track/road to the right immediately, and keep left at the Y-fork after 100m/yds. When, after about 10 minutes, the tarmac ends at a Y-fork (❻; **1h45min**), keep straight ahead (left) on the main track. Continue uphill until you go over a crest, then fork right downhill and, after passing a SMALLHOLDING in the trees, descend to a tarmac road (slightly downhill to your right). Turn right on this road and follow it back down to the junction by VILLA THEA where you parked (❶; **2h55min**). If you came by bus, retrace your steps to the MARKET and BUS STOP at **Sgombou** (❶).

Walk 21: DOUKADES AND AG SIMEON

Distance/time: 3.4km/2.2mi; 1h15min; 5km/3mi; 1h35min for bus users
Grade: ● fairly easy, but with a steep climb of 175m/750ft to Ag Simeon (225m/0000ft for bus users) — and little shade when you get there
Equipment: stout shoes with good ankle support or walking trainers, sunhat, suncream, sunglasses, picnic, water
Picnic suggestion: Ag Simeon
Access: 🚗 to/from Doukades; park in the upper parking area, above the square (39° 41.432'N, 19° 44.428'E) and walk down to the square; or Paleokastritsa 🚌 to the Doukades turn-off 200m east of the petrol station, below the village (**ⓐ**; adds 20min overall and 50m of ascent/descent)

Y ou climb an escarpment to the precariously-perched chapel of Ag Simeon, overlooking the turquoise waters of Liapades Bay. A striking panorama spreads out below you, overlooking the central hills and the coast.

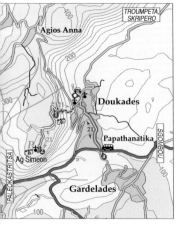

German, 'ZUR KAPELLE', here). Turn off up the first narrow lane on the right. Leave the houses, following a cobbled path straight uphill (it may be covered in brushwood at first, and hard to locate). Within the first minute you cross a galvanised water pipe at an intersection, where you continue straight on, climbing steeply. When you meet a concrete lane (**❶**), turn left uphill. The lane soon becomes a stony track.

Start the walk at the SQUARE in **Doukades** (**O**): with your back to the Taverna Dukas and its pretty patio with benches and a small tree, walk downhill between two bar/tavernas: Elizabeth (left) and To Steki (right). After 50m/yds the road curves left: go right here, up a wide alley surfaced with crazy-paving. Follow this for 50m to a junction, where you turn right. Walk alongside a walled-in villa, with the front door of a CHURCH to your right.

Cross a road and continue up the path (there may be a sign in

On the ascent you have stupendous views over Doukades, towards a valley clad in silvery-grey olive groves pierced with the dark spires of cypress trees. There used to be wonderful views from the crest of the escarpment, but scrub has all but blocked them out. Don't worry — a superb panorama awaits you later at Ag Simeon. About 10 minutes along the track you reach an unsigned fork. Take the left-hand fork; this descends gently at first, then soon rises. At the end of the track you're looking down on the chapel from the vantage point shown opposite. A minute down, at **Ag Simeon** (❷; **40min**), a superb cliff-top panorama awaits you. Liapades is the larger village across from you; Gardelades is to the left. The Ropa Plain, a carpet of green in spring, slides into the central hills. In the distance, beyond the rolling wooded hills, sits Corfu Town. Paleokastritsa lies among the prominent headlands below.

After a break and perhaps a picnic, return the same way to the SQUARE in **Doukades** (❶; **1h15min**). Be sure to amble round this charming village before leaving.

Typical Corfiot alleyway with white crazy-paving

Walk 22: AG GEORGIOS AND MIRTIOTISSA CIRCUIT

Distance/time: 6.7km/4.2mi; 2h35min

Grade: ● moderate-strenuous, ups and downs of about 400m/ 1300ft; stony paths, little shade

Equipment: boots or stout shoes with good ankle support, sunhat, suncream, sunglasses, swimwear, picnic, plenty of water

Picnic suggestions: Ag Georgios

Access: 🚗 to/from Kelia: from the golf club entrance at Vatos head east for 'KERKYRA' (Corfu Town). Pass the petrol station on the right and turn right uphill for 'VATOS 1'. The road turns sharp right and comes to a church on the right. Turn *left* opposite this church. After 350m park by a walled-in cemetery on the left (39° 36.290'N, 19° 47.829'E). *Early-birds could park at the foot of the Mirtiotissa lane, to avoid climbing at the end of the walk.* Or Glyfada 🚌 to the Kelia turn-off (adds 200m each way).

While Mirtiotissa is no longer the idyllic setting so beloved of Lawrence Durrell — storms have carried away much of the sand — it is still very beautiful and a welcome break after the ascent of Ag Georgios. Be aware that Mirtiotissa is now a (very popular) naturist beach.

Start the walk from the WALLED CEMETERY (**O**). (Bus users head back west from the Kelia turn-off (**a**) the way the bus has come; you will come to the cemetery in just over 200m.) Walk west from the cemetery for just 70m/yds, to **Kelia**, and turn left on a paved path past SPIROS TAVERNA. Continue up a path through olive groves to a lane, where you turn left. This climbs steadily on the lower flanks of **Mt Ag Georgios**. Shortly after passing two RADIO MASTS, turn right up a path signed 'ST GEORGE' (**❶**). This is a very pleasant climb through rock roses. You look down onto a beryl sea, as the hillside plummets to the rocks below. The tiny eponymous chapel at the SUMMIT of **Ag Georgios** dates from the 12th century (**❷**; **1h05min**). What a vantage point! You have a 360° view taking in the whole of Corfu and stretching out past Corfu Town to Albania.

Mirtiotissa: the beach is narrower now than when this photo was taken.

When you've had your fill of views, go back down to the lane (**❶**; **1h20min**) and turn right. Don't forget to look back for spectacular views along the hilly coastline. Fifteen minutes into the descent, the track forks. Descend to the left, passing the

scant remains of the abandoned hamlet of **Trialos** (❸). Dropping gently downhill, keep a chain link fence on your left. At the bottom of the path, at the end of the fence and near the cliff-top, turn left through a gap in the fence along a narrow but well defined path. Now not far above the cliffs, you come upon a view southwards along the coast. Further on, the path widens to a track again, and the building high up on your left is **Moni Mirtiotissa** (❹). Continue along the track to the turn-off up to the fenced and gated monastery. If the solitary monk is in residence, and if you are properly dressed, you should be able to visit the church, which is packed with interesting artifacts.

Leaving the monastery, walk down to **Mirtiotissa Beach** (❺; **1h50min**), backed by towering pine-clad cliffs. From late autumn until spring attractive streamlets cascade down these rocky walls, and the beach is as

idyllic as it looks in the photo below. But in summer it's packed out, and you may not see the sand for beach umbrellas… or bodies.

The ascent back up from the beach is a bit of a slog. You pass a taverna on the right: follow the rough lane for another 400m, to where the road bends 90° right. Almost at once, where it bends left again, turn left on a TRACK (later a path; ❻) which takes you back down to the WALLED-IN CEMETERY (**O**; **2h35min**). Bus users turn right here, back to the Kelia junction BUS STOP (ⓐ).

Walk 23: ACROSS THE ISLAND TO MIRTIOTISSA

See also photographs on pages
93, 96-97,102-103
Distance/time: 13.8km/8.5mi;
3h50min
Grade: ● moderate, with an
ascent of 200m/650ft above
Vatos and a steep descent of
50m/150ft on the last stretch to
the beach at Glyfada
Equipment: walking boots or
shoes with good grip, sunhat,
sunglasses, suncream, raingear,
long-sleeved shirt, long trousers,
swimwear, picnic, water
Picnic suggestions: Scotini
Pond, Mirtiotissa Beach
Access: 🚌 to Gouvia, journey

time 20min). Alight just before
traffic lights on the dual carriageway, diagonally opposite Diella's
Supermarket (a huge green
building). Return on 🚌 from
Glyfada; journey time 40min
**Shorter walk: Scotini Pond and
the Ropa Plain.** 8.25km/ 5mi;
2h10min. ● Easy; stout shoes
will suffice; access by 🚌 as main
walk; return by bus from Vatos
(Glyfada bus). Follow the main
walk to Vatos and keep on the
main road past the petrol station.
Catch the bus at the Pelekas/
Glyfada junction, on the Corfu
Town side of the road.

Cross the island from east to west and discover the
diversity of Corfu's landscapes. Within a stone's throw
of Gouvia's tourist haunts, you're in the countryside. Half
an hour brings you to quiet rolling hills. You come upon
a large pond full of terrapin and frogs, in an enchanting
valley. Heading west, you cross the Ropa Plain — with a
mere scattering of trees, it sits like an airfield, buried below
hills. Ascending the slopes of Mt Ag Georgios, the west
coast unravels — in complete contrast to the east. Vivid
green pines fleck the rocky sea-cliffs towering above some
of the island's most beautiful beaches — the most
spectacular being Mirtiotissa.

Start the walk at the BUS STOP in
Gouvia (○), on the main dual
carriageway just before the traffic
lights — and a huge green 'landmark' building: DIELLA'S SUPER-
MARKET on the left. Cross the
road carefully then skirt the left
side of Diella's on a country road
(do *not* turn left on the road to
Danilia, the folklore village).
After 700m, at the fourth turn-
off left, there are signs for some
villas, among them 'JASMIN' and
'AGLAIA' (❶; **10min**): turn left
here. Keep to this lane for just
under 1km; then, on crossing a
low crest, take the *second* turning
down to the left, a roughly

concreted track. You pass a
house on your right. Skirting a
fenced-off field, descend into a
gentle open valley. Five minutes
off the road, you're overlooking
Scotini (❸), the pond shown
opposite — unless it's high
summer!
A minute past the pond, head left
at a junction. Ignore a fork to the
left almost immediately and soon
reach a ROAD (**40min**). Turn left
and, four minutes along (after
400m), turn sharp right on a
side-road, soon passing a few
country villas in nice gardens.
Some 600m further on, at a
junction, fork right (slightly

Scotini Pond

uphill). Continue along this road for 700m, then turn 90° left on a gravel track (there may be a sign, 'VATOS-ROPA', on the gateway of a small market garden on the right). You soon pass a house on the right, behind a wall, with a SHRINE in the garden.

Soon you're descending into the **Ropa Valley**. Just after ignoring a faint farm track off to the right, come to a junction, where a WIDE TRACK (**④**) cuts across in front of you: follow it to the right. The Ropa Valley begins appearing in bits and pieces, over the trees. Gianades is the village visible midway up the Marmaro Hills, across the plain. Five-six minutes from the junction (after 650m

you join a road coming from the right. Keep left here and pass a few houses. A working QUARRY has eaten away half of the hillside on the left. Five minutes along the road, you emerge on the quarry road and turn right. Minutes down you're on the CORFU/LIAPADES ROAD (**1h35min**), where you turn right.

From here you cross the **Ropa Plain**. Some 40m/yds along the road, turn left on a FARM TRACK (**⑤**) that strikes across the plain. In spring the grass is knee-high and full of flowers. Looking ahead, you can see the village of Vatos, your next objective, strung out along the lower slopes

105

of Mt Ag Georgios. Some 20 minutes along, you reach another wide DRAINAGE DITCH (**6**). At this point you join the CORFU TRAIL (southbound) and you will be with it as far as Mirtiotissa. It's likely that you'll spot some birds now: crested larks, red storks, goldfinches, stonechats, whinchats. Turn left and keep along the bank, with the wide ditch on your right. You soon join a gravel track (the ditch now almost resembling a canal), and you will pass several steel bridges linking the golf course on each side the canal. Keep along the track, cross a concrete slab bridge, and soon pass the GOLF COURSE CLUBHOUSE on the opposite bank. When you meet the ERMONES ROAD, close to the entrance to the golf club, on the outskirts of **Vatos** (**2h05min**), turn left.

Two minutes along (less than 100m past a PETROL STATION), turn right on a narrow tarred road (**7**). *(The Shorter walk keeps ahead 300m to the Pelekas/Glyfada junction and a bus stop.)* A couple of minutes uphill, the road veers sharply left, in front of a house. Some 30m/yds beyond the house, go right on a path bordered by high fences. Following this old village path, you come out on a village road, five minutes from the main road. Head left, then right, following the CORFU TRAIL along an alley into the TOP PART OF **Vatos** (**2h20min**). After 160m/yds take the next road on the right (with an information board at its start). It doubles back momentarily, passes the village school, and

heads uphill. This lane, later a track, climbs steadily on the lower flanks of **Mt Ag Georgios**. Shortly after passing two RADIO MASTS, you join Walk 22 at the 1h20min-point in that walk. Pick up the notes on page 102 and follow that walk to **Mirtiotissa Beach** (**8**; **3h20min**).

Heading on to Glyfada, follow the steep track from Mirtiotissa Beach. Close on 10 minutes uphill, just after an S-bend and once through the car park of the roadside TAVERNA, descend a track on your right (**9**). This runs through a grove of olive trees, towards a restaurant/bar set back in the trees (closed at time of writing). Keep to the left of a small toilet block and take the path ahead, running between two fences. *(Do not* descend to the right.) Crossing a small flat area, you overlook Glyfada's wide beach — another stupendous setting below cliffs studded with beautiful, fluffy pines. But alas, a large hotel and apartment blocks have blighted its natural beauty.

Dropping down off this flat-topped clearing, you follow a watercourse and drop very steeply downhill. Take care, as the descent is stony. Three minutes down you emerge at the back of a restaurant. From here, descend steps at the side of the restaurant to the BEACH at **Glyfada** (**3h40min**). Head along the beach to the left for five minutes, then ascend a wide road to a large car park. Continue up the road for five minutes, to the junction above the hotel, where the bus turns around (**O**; **3h50min**).

Walk 24: THREE WALKS TO MONI PANTOKRATOR OF AG DEKA

See also photo on page 40

Walk a for bus users (Ano Garouna to Benitses)

Distance/time: 7km/4.5mi; 2h25min

Grade: ● moderate; ascent of 280m/920ft and steep descent of 580m/1900ft, sometimes on steps; agility required

Equipment: walking boots, sunhat, sunglasses, suncream, long-sleeved shirt, long trousers (protection from thorny scrub as well as the sun), fleece, raingear, swimwear, picnic, water

Picnic suggestions: Moni Pantokrator, waterworks garden

Access: 🚌 to Ano Garouna; journey time 40min. Return on 🚌 from Benitses; journey time 30min

Walk b for motorists (Circuit from Makrata)

Distance/time: 8.6km/5.3mi; 3h

Grade: ● moderate; ascents/descents of 500m/1650ft; steep paths and steps require agility

Equipment/Picnic: as Walk a (except for swimwear)

Access: 🚗 to/from Makrata; park at the crossroads (39° 32.374'N, 19° 53.849'E)

Walk c for motorists or bus users (Ag Deka out-and-back)

3.5km/2mi; 1h25min. ● Moderate ups/downs of 280m/920ft. Equipment/access as Walk a; return on the same bus. Or 🚗 to the car park below Ano Garouna (39° 32.831'N, 19° 52.235'E). Follow WALK A to the 45min-point (❷) and return the same way.

Ag Deka, Corfu's second-highest peak (576m/1890ft), is a pint-sized mountain rising in the centre of the island. A radar station means the summit is out of bounds, but that doesn't matter. Far more appealing is the shallow depression on the mountaintop — the crater of an ancient volcano according to folklore. It's a rival for the Garden of Eden — an unkempt orchard boasting some 45 different varieties of fruits. And tucked away behind creepered walls sits Moni Pantokrator of Ag Deka, a cool, shady sanctuary. These three walks offer magnificent panoramas of the inland hills and vales edging out to the coasts, before they tumble into the sea. Walks a and b share part of the route with the Corfu Trail, and both visit an enchanting overgrown garden at the foot of Ag Deka — a waterworks, built almost 200 years ago to supply Corfu Town with water.

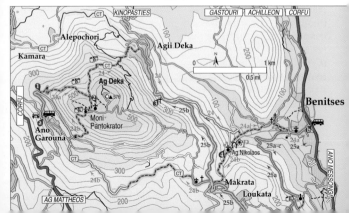

Start Walk a at the BUS SHELTER/ CAR PARKING AREA (**a**) below **Ano Garouna**. Facing the bus shelter, head up the road to the right, keeping right at a fork. After 500m/yds, after a U-bend to the right, fork left on a concrete and gravel track with a walkers' signpost, 'To PANTO-KRATOR' (**1**). When the track ends, continue on the path that leads off it. The path is always distinct, but you may have to push your way through encroaching vegetation. As you climb your views expand as far north as Pantokrator. A steady ascent brings you to a JUNCTION (**40min**).

The village of Ag Deka (visited later in the walk) is down to the left; Moni Pantokrator of Ag Deka is up to the right. Head right, joining the **CORFU TRAIL**. Passing an orchard of cherry and walnut trees, you enter the court-yard of **Moni Pantokrator** (**2**; **45min**). You are now in the shallow 'crater', but perhaps unaware of it. The chapel is usually locked; the monks' quarters are now used only for storage, or when a local festivity takes grip of the site. You can quench your thirst at the well — unless it, too, is locked.

Before continuing the walk, head over to the access road and the CHAPEL in a clearing at the edge of the mountain for some fabulous views. Then return to the junction below the *moni* and keep straight on (right) for the village of Ag Deka, still on the **CORFU TRAIL**. Ten minutes down this partly-cobbled path you pass a prominent rock — an excellent viewpoint. You look

Gathering chestnuts in autumn at Moni Pantokrator of Ag Deka

straight down onto the lagoon near the airport — a view similar to the one shown on page 40. Villages encircled by olive groves lie scattered amidst the hills. The prominent white building down to the right is Achilleion Palace. Soon reaching a stone and earth track, turn left downhill. Round an S-bend and keep descending. Two minutes down the track, turn sharp right on a narrower track. Then, after just 50m/yds, watch for a boulder with a red arrow: this alerts you to your ongoing path which drops steeply down to the left, with olive trees up to your right and a chain link fence on the left. Keep descending, following the fence round to the left (where another path joins from the right). Some 20m/yds downhill, turn right (with another fence on your left). Cross a water pipe and continue downhill, shortly descending some rough steps leading down to a parking area. Turn right immediately above

the car park, along a concrete path leading in less than 100m/yds into the VILLAGE OF **Ag Deka**. Keep ahead along the narrow alleys, and in three minutes you will emerge on the road (**1h25min**).

Turn right on the road, *leaving* the CORFU TRAIL (which heads left). A good five minutes along, as you leave the village and just after rounding a bend, you pass a LARGE SHRINE (**❸**) built into a retaining wall round a small park on the left. Some 40m/yds past the shrine turn left downhill on a two-wheel track. On the descent ignore the steep track off right after 1km but, about 150m further on, when you come to a well-kept garden on the left, turn right on a path. Then turn right again at the T-junction that follows. In two minutes you're at the wild, wild WATERWORKS GARDEN (**❹**; **2h**) shown overleaf. A stream runs down the valley floor, which is a lush, exuberant tangle of vegetation. An intriguing old TUNNEL further upstream was once part of an aqueduct.

Return to the T-junction and now keep straight on, past orchards and vegetable gardens. A railed walkway takes you to a road. Walk right along the road for a minute, to two SHRINES ahead, then descend steps alongside the first of the SHRINES. Follow the road below the shrine for a few metres; then, head left on a path into the trees, opposite a house on the right with yellow-brick cladding. This path emerges on the road to the WATER TREATMENT WORKS. Turn right down the concrete road for 40m/yds, then turn left down a path opposite the gated entrance to the works.

Passing a CEMETERY, you join a narrow road at a tree-shaded PARKING AREA next to a stream. Cross the stream and continue along a narrow street through the old village. This leads you to the MAIN SQUARE at **Benitses**,

The luxuriant waterworks garden hidden behind touristic Benitses

opposite the HARBOUR
(**2h25min**). A BUS SHELTER is
ahead (**ⓑ**). You can take any bus
(green or blue) on the sea side of
the main road.
Start Walk b at the **Makrata**
CROSSROADS (**ⓒ**) by following
the **CORFU TRAIL** west on a
concrete road signed 'TO
PANTOKRATOR'. After a SHRINE
and then a CHAPEL the right, turn
left on a two wheeled track in
front of a low brick wall. This
becomes a mossy wooded path
through old olive groves and
then runs into a surfaced track
which rises steadily.
When you meet a minor road by
some houses, turn left. Then take
the first right and continue in the

same direction (at the left of a
house) on a wide grassy path.
The stiff climb through
woodland brings you to a
CHAPEL at the edge of the
mountain with fine views and
then to **Moni Pantokrator** (**❷**;
1h30min).
From the monastery follow
WALK A from the 45min-point
(**❷**), adding 45 minutes to all
time checks. When you reach the
WATERWORKS GARDEN, head
upstream to a TUNNEL and take
the steps behind it up to the
Ag Nikolaos CHAPEL (**❹**). Then
continue quite steeply uphill,
near a stream, to a concrete lane
and then the **Makrata** crossroads
(**ⓒ**; **3h**).

Walk 25: FOUR WALKS TO MONI PANTOKRATOR OF STAVROS

See map opposite; see also photograph on page 40

Distance/time, Grade, Return transport: see Walks a-d below

Equipment: walking boots or stout shoes with grip and ankle support, sunhat, sunglasses, suncream, long-sleeved shirt, long trousers, fleece, raingear, swimwear, picnic, water

Picnic suggestion: Komianata: above or below the village

Access (Walks a-c): 🚌 to Benitses; park in the seafront car park (39° 32.848'N, 19° 54.776'E). Or 🚍; journey time 30min

Walk a: Circuit from Benitses to Moni Pantokrator

Distance/time: 9.5km/6mi; 3h35min

Grade: ● strenuous; ascent of 400m/1300ft and descent of 400m/1300ft (dangerous if wet)

Return: 🚌 or 🚍 from Benitses

Walk b: Pantokrator circuit including Ag Deka village

Distance/time: 14.6km/9.1mi; 4h20min

Grade/Return: ● as Walk a

Walk c: Benitses to Strongili via Moni Pantokrator

Distance/time: 10km/6.25mi; 3h20min

Grade: ● as Walk a

Return: 🚍 from Strongili; journey time 1h

Walk d: Circuit from Komianata to Moni Pantokrator

3.8km/2.4mi; 1h20min. ● Moderate; overall ascent 100m/330ft; some paths are very rocky.

Access: Strongili 🚍 or 🚌 to/from Komianata; park just before the road ends (39° 31.756'N, 19° 54.355'E), *don't block the bus turning bay!* Follow Walks a-c from the 1h15min-point to the 2h35min-point page 112).

W inding up through cypresses and olive groves, Walks a-c climb from Benitses to the hillside village of Dafnata, trailing superb coastal scenery. The village sits high and fast on table-topped Mt Stavros. Across the mountain stands yet another little Moni Pantokrator. Before we reach it, we pick up Walk d — and the Corfu Trail — at Komianata.

Walks a-c follow the same route to Moni Pantokrator. **Start out** from the CAR PARK/BUS SHELTER at **Benitses** (**O**): head inland and cross the square, following signs for 'OLD VILLAGE' and a Chinese restaurant. Turn left in front of a yellow-brick taverna, then right (same signs). Go left at a Y-fork, passing the Chinese restaurant on the left and a yellow CHURCH on the right. At the Y-fork past the church, go right downhill and cross a BRIDGE. You arrive at a CAR PARK and JUNCTION (**❶**).

Take the second turning left, a sealed track. Follow this gently uphill for a good 1.5 kilometres, then turn right on the drive up to a CHAPEL (**❷**), where a cool, refreshing spring in the shade of an enormous oak tree awaits you. Follow the path below the chapel courtyard, heading round the hillside and crossing a dry stream bed. After five minutes, the path climbs to a tarmac road. Turn right on this road and, where it bends left, there is a lovely view down over Benitses and along the coast to Corfu Town.

Continue uphill through pine woods and, when the road enters an olive grove, *watch out* for a path on the left. Follow this path steeply uphill through cypress trees. Five minutes up, watch for a fork and head right, steeply uphill, on a zigzag path. When you meet a track, follow it to the right; it soon becomes a concrete lane leading you steeply up to the road at **Dafnata** — where there is a lovely viewpoint overlooking Corfu Town and the east coast. An old millstone acts as a table, and there are several seats. Turn left along the road through the village, to the hamlet of **Komianata**. Continue straight ahead along an alley to the tiny square, with a small tree in the middle (**❸; 1h15min**). *(Walk d joins here.)*

As soon as you enter the square, take the first path left uphill (at the *top* of the square). Then turn right immediately, making your way behind the houses, to begin the ascent of Mt Stavros. Soon there is a superb outlook across the centre of the island — making this a lovely, shady place to picnic. Two minutes along the path (about 150m), ignore a turn-off to the right (your return route). Instead do a short zigzag uphill by turning left; then, after a few metres, go right, continuing uphill. Your destination is the hilltop slightly to the right. Ignore another, faint fork to the left barely two minutes later. Keep beside a fenced-off area, rounding the hillside. When you reach a track, turn right and follow it across the shoulder of **Mt Stavros**, ignoring tracks left and right.

Soon after passing between some hillside vegetable plots, the track begins to descend and you will shortly spot **Moni Pantokrator** (**❹; 2h**) below you on the right. The building stands on a rocky outcrop at the end of the track, hanging out over the Messongi Valley. Inside the chapel are some barely-discernible frescoes and a fine canvas.

Before heading on, get your bearings. Facing the track, look left, to see your return route below, running along the slopes of Mt Stavros. Then head back up the track for 25m/yds and take a path descending to the left (beside a large rock). Ignore a fork off left two minutes down. Circling the mountainside, you catch sight of Strongili below. Half an hour from the chapel, ignore a faint turn-off to the left. (It's a short-cut to the Strongili route below, but is overgrown.) Coming into olive groves again, keep uphill to the right, soon rejoining your outgoing path, where you turn left. Two minutes down, you're back at the square in **Komianata** (**❸; 2h35min**). *(Walk d finishes here; 1h20min.)*

Walk a retraces steps from here to **Dafnata** and then back to **Benitses** (**○; 3h35min**).

Walk b retraces steps from here to **Dafnata**, but then follows the road (and the CORFU TRAIL) through **Halidata**. After just under 2km you reach the AG DEKA/STRONGILI road at **Makrata** (**❺**). Turn right and follow it to the southern outskirts of **Ag Deka** village. Just as you approach the first house on the right, turn *sharp* right down a two-wheel track. (If you pass a LARGE SHRINE on the left (**❻**) built into a retaining wall, you have gone 40m too far.)

Moni Pantokrator of Stavros

Now pick up WALK 24 on page 109, *and note that the waypoint numbering differs from Walk 25.* Follow WALK 24 from just after the 1h25min-point to the WATERWORKS GARDEN and then on to the BUS SHELTER and CAR PARKING AREA in **Benitses** (**○**; **4h20min**).

Walk c descends from the square at **Komianata** (**❸**) to Strongili: first head left from the bottom of the square, following a YELLOW CORFU TRAIL ARROW. A stony track takes you down into cypresses (another lovely picnic setting with plenty of shade). Keep to the main route, passing some iron sheds on your right and ignoring any turnings to the right. Ten minutes from the square (well under 1km), above a roofless stone building down to the right, keep left at a fork. At the next fork, five minutes later, go right.

Shortly, Strongili reappears. Five minutes from the last fork, you pass a CHAPEL (**❼**) on your right, meet a track and follow it to the left. The track forks immediately: keep right downhill. In five minutes, when the track forks again, go right and, metres downhill, go left on a path (YELLOW ARROW ON A TREE). Passing an abandoned CHAPEL on your left, the path runs to the right of a GATE and FENCED-OFF ORANGE GROVE. Meeting a track close to the village CHURCH and CEMETERY (**❽**), follow it to the STRONGILI ROAD. Turn left into **Strongili** (**❾**; **3h20min**), where there is a choice of cafés and a BUS STOP.

Walk 26: TWO WALKS FROM HLOMOS

See also photograph page 32

Walk a: Linear route recommended for bus users. Messongi — Hlomos — Petreti — Perivoli

Distance/time: 14km/8.7mi; 4h
Grade: ● easy-moderate, with a steep ascent of 300m/1000ft at the start (on a road)
Equipment: stout shoes, sunhat, sunglasses, suncream, long-sleeved shirt, long trousers, rain-gear, swimwear, picnic, water
Picnic suggestions: church balcony at Hlomos, Korakades or Notos
Access: 🚌 to Messongi (or Kavos bus to Messongi); journey time 45min; or 🚗 to Messongi; park along the seafront, inside the village, at the side of the road near the bus stop (39° 28.664'N, 19° 56.018'E). Return on 🚌 from Perivoli; journey time 1h05min, back to Corfu Town, or to your car at Messongi

Walk b: Circuit recommended for motorists. Hlomos — Petreti — Boukari — Hlomos

Distance/time: 11.5km/7.1mi; 2h45min
Grade: ● easy-moderate; overall descent/ascent of 220m/ 720ft
Equipment/Picnic as for Walk a
Access: 🚗 to/from Hlomos: park in the car park by the bus stop at the entrance to the village (39° 27.307'N, 19° 57.369'E). Or 🚌 to/from Hlomos; journey time 1h15min

These walks may not appeal to everyone because of the road-walking. But outside peak season they carry only a trickle of traffic, and several users have told us how much they enjoyed the linear walk. Charming villages and hamlets lie on route; each has its own personality. They adorn ridges, step hillsides, and dribble down slopes to the sea. You wind your way around the sylvan, seaward slopes, through olive groves and down lanes of cypress trees. Seascapes ebb and flow.

Walk a: Start out at the BUS STOP/TURNAROUND (ⓐ) in **Messongi**. Walk back the way the bus came into the village and, at the crossroads (**2min**), turn left towards Ag Dimitrios (not signed when last checked). Mt Ag Mattheos (Walk 27) rises straight ahead of you. Follow the road uphill past Kato Spilion, a small village on a side-road off to the right. On arriving on the outskirts of **Ag Dimitrios** (**55min**), the road swings left to Hlomos. But before heading along it, continue up to the right towards the village centre for a minute — to enjoy a superb panorama encompassing the central mountains, the gulf and the Pantokrator hills. Returning to the Hlomos road, follow it for a little under 1km, then take first turn-off left (signposted 'CHURCH OF ARCHANGELS') — up to the top of this cascading village. Two minutes up, turn right along a lane; it curves left, passing below the church. From the CHURCH at **Hlomos** (Ⓞ; **1h20min**) there are fine views along the northern coastline to Mt Pantokrator, and south to the tip of the island. It's a pleasant picnic spot.

Leaving the church, head back along the lane, then take the first alley off left, following a sign for

114

TAVERNA SIRTAKI. Old houses flank the alley. A minute down, either head right to the taverna or turn left and then go right immediately, to descend to the village square, a minute below. On reaching the narrow square, continue straight downhill. (Coming from the taverna, this is the first right turn out of the square.) Half a minute down from the square, descend steps to the right, then continue along the track, down into a gully. The way heads along the side of a steep embankment. *Keep an eye out for old red and blue dot waymarks.* Eight minutes down, at a fork just past a shed on the right, keep left. Two minutes later, keep right at the next fork. A minute later, by another shed, go right (both branches end up

in the same place, but the left-hand track is overgrown). Soon you meet another track (just where it veers off to the left). Continue straight ahead along this track. Just after a fork off to the right, at a junction, again continue straight on, ignoring the fork to the left. You pass through **Kouspades** (**2h**), a picture-postcard village. At a junction just past the pretty BELL-TOWER go right (**❶**). (Walk 26b comes in from the left at this junction.) Then, at the next junction 80m/yds further on, take the second left. Some five minutes later, pass through **Vassilatika**.

Continue along the road into **Korakades**, where you turn right along the village lane. An air of abandon hangs over this farming

The balcony at Hlomos church, decorated for Easter

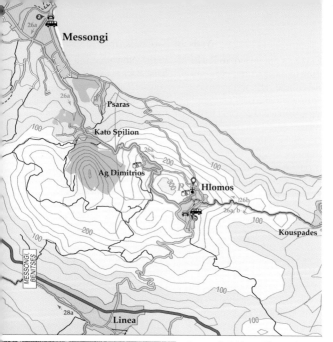

Painted stone outside the village

settlement. Soon the lane veers sharp left. Descending past derelict houses, you wind your way down the hillside, with tremendous views over the rooftops onto the Lefkimmi flats and the hills of Epirus. It's another nice picnic spot, where you can sit on the wall at the side of the road, in the shade of olive trees.

A good 10 minutes down, meet a ROAD (**②**) on the outskirts of the small fishing village of **Petreti**. Cross the road and continue downhill on a lane more or less opposite. A minute later, you cross the road again. At the bottom of the lane, turn left. Then, 100m/yds along, take the lane forking off right, down to a mud-flat beach (**2h55min**). Now turn right along the seafront and continue along the beach, crossing two streams (no footbridges). At the far end of the beach, follow a path through an olive grove over a low headland and on to the pretty cove of **Notos** (**③**). This quiet, little-frequented port makes another pleasant picnic spot, with shade nearby. Climb a short concrete lane, to join a tarmac road at the crest. Continue along the coast road and, 10 minutes later, at a T-junction, turn left, still following the coast. Just 1km from the T-junction, bythe pretty harbour at **Kaliviotes**, the road turns inland, to Perivoli (**4h**). The BUS STOP (❹) is in front of the cafés and bars, just to the right of the T-junction.

Walk b: From the BUS STOP/ CAR PARK at **Hlomos** (ⓑ), continue

off left. Now use the notes for WALK A from the 1h20min-point until you reach the cove of **Notos**.

Then return around the headland to **Petreti**. Cross the beach, pass

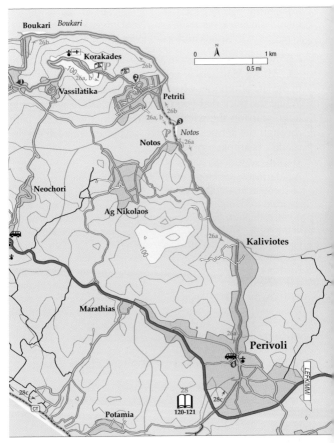

straight ahead past a 'no through road' sign, to the narrow village 'SQUARE'. You will continue from here by taking the first right turn out of the square, but first make your way up to the CHURCH (●), a pleasant picnic spot with lovely views.

Then **start the walk**: from the CHURCH head back along the lane below and take the first alley

the FISHING HARBOUR, and take the road along the coast. Follow this for 2km, to arrive at sandy **Boukari Beach**. From here follow the road up to **Kouspades** and, at the top of the hill, turn right (❶) and pass the pretty BELL TOWER on your left. Now retrace your outgoing route back to the CAR PARK at **Hlomos** (ⓑ; **2h45min**).

Walk 27: MT AG MATTHEOS

Distance/time: 6km/3.75mi; 2h05min
Grade: ● strenuous; ascent of 300m/1000ft on a motorable track and a descent of 300m/1000ft on a rocky path and track
Equipment: walking boots, sunhat, sunglasses, suncream, long-sleeved shirt, long trousers, raingear, picnic, plenty of water
Access: 🚗 to/from the edge of Ag Mattheos; park on the main road south of the village, at the 5min-point in the walk, near the 'gnome' garden (39° 29.505'N, 19° 52.773'E). Or 🚌 to/from Ag Mattheos village centre; journey time 50min

The panoramic view over the south of the island from Mt Ag Mattheos is well worth the climb. It's best done in the late afternoon, when it's cooler and the light is softer. While the track that you follow on the ascent is wide and ugly, scarring the whole mountainside, the descent path through the kermes oak wood (one of the few left on the island), is ample compensation.

Start the walk in the village of **Ag Mattheos**, outside the cafés on the MAIN ROAD (**O**). Follow the main road south for a little over five minutes. Near the end of the village, just past a house on the right, turn right up a lane signposted 'MONASTERY OF PANTOKRATOR'. As soon as you turn off you'll spot a GARDEN WITH GNOMES (**❶**) — Snow White and the Seven Dwarfs! Ignore the turn-off to the right soon afterwards. Soon concrete comes underfoot, then gravel. Another road and a track join from the right within the first 10 minutes: continue straight uphill. At the next fork, at a metal barrier, go straight on (to the left is the original mountain track, now partly bulldozed away).

Ascending, there is a good outlook over the thickly-wooded Messongi basin below. Higher up, you enjoy a bird's-eye view over the village of Ag Mattheos, then Messongi Bay. The east coast slowly unravels and, on a bend, you look out over the Korission Lagoon (**50min**).

Mt Ag Mattheos rises in the background in this photo taken at the sand dunes near Issos Beach (Walk 28, Car tour 4) — a good picnic spot.

Attractive houses — like this one at Ag Mattheos — are a strong feature of Corfu's landscape.

Soon the kermes oak wood closes in around you and concrete comes underfoot.

Just below the summit you reach **Moni Pantokrator** (❷; **1h 10min**). Standing on the track below the walled compound, pick up the path that climbs to the left of the *moni* and to THREE RATHER DILAPIDATED LOOKOUT POINTS (❸), the first with a hut on stilts overlooking the west coast. Continue beyond the trig point in a ruined walled enclosure at the SUMMIT OF **Mt Ag Mattheos** to a seat overlooking the east coast and another seat further on, with southerly views to both coasts and Lake Korission. In October the rocky hilltop is a mass of cyclamen and crocuses, and tiny goldcrests and redstarts flit about the wood, while the occasional buzzard circles overhead.

Head back down past the *moni*. Pass a small tiled building on the right, then pick up a path which disappears into the woods. Five minutes along, ignore a path to the right. Leaving the cover of trees, the north of the island comes into view. Less than 40 minutes down, you emerge on a bend of your outgoing track (**1h50min**).

Follow the track to the left for 45m/yds, then turn left down another track, through an olive grove. Continue round to the right, downhill, when concrete comes underfoot. A little over five minutes off the mountain track, you're in the SQUARE in **Ag Mattheos**. Walk right, past the CHURCH (❹), then take the first left and next right. Then follow a narrow lane downhill to the main road, just to the left of the cafés (**2h05min**).

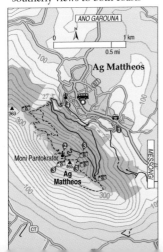

119

Walk 28: THREE WALKS AT LAKE KORISSION

See also photos pages 32, 118
Distance/time, Grade, Access:
see Walks a-c below
Equipment: trainers, sunhat, sunglasses, suncream, swimwear,
picnic, plenty of water
Picnic: anywhere en route!

Walk a: Lake Korission circuit

Distance/time: 16km/10mi;
4h40min
Grade: ● easy, but *very* long; *no*
shade on the beaches
Access: 🚌 to/from Halikouna

Beach (39° 27.165'N, 19° 52.581'E)

Walk b: Gardiki Castle to Argirades

Distance/time: 15km/9.5mi; 4h
Grade: ● easy; mostly along a
beach … but plodding over sand is
tiring. Steep climb of 100m/330ft
to Argirades. *Almost no shade*
Access: 🚌 to the Gardiki turn-off
(Ag Mattheos bus); journey time
45min. Return by 🚌 from Argirades (journey time 1h)
See below for Walk 28c

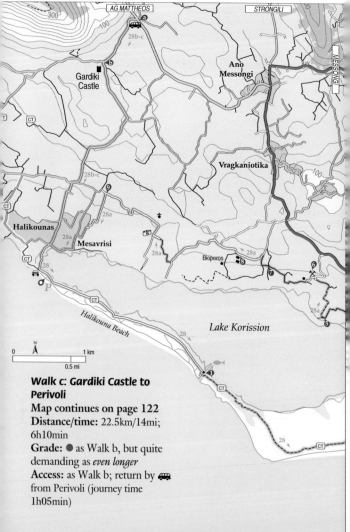

Walk c: Gardiki Castle to Perivoli

Map continues on page 122
Distance/time: 22.5km/14mi;
6h10min
Grade: ● as Walk b, but quite
demanding as *even longer*
Access: as Walk b; return by 🚌
from Perivoli (journey time
1h05min)

Here are three splendid, very long walks — one a circuit especially suitable for motorists and two hikes for bus users. But any of the three can be shortened by judicious use of the map, and all three are suitable for out-and-about leg stretchers — perhaps with a picnic. All three follow the seashore initially — a seemingly endless sandy beach. 'Lake' Korission is a shallow lagoon bordered by a causeway of sand dunes. Traipsing across the dunes you pass through an enchanting thicket of holly oak, a pretty interlude before you come upon the *real* dunes — billows of golden sand splashed with silver-green clumps of juniper. Fish was farmed at the lake in Venetian times, and a canal was cut through to join the lake to the sea.

Walk a is highly recommended for its variety and some shade in the second, inland half. When you come back to the sea at the end, you can really relax on the beach, knowing that your car is nearby. Walks b and c leave the dunes behind; you paddle along below sandstone banks that soon grow into cliffs, and you return to deserted beaches, before climbing back to the main road for a bus.

Walk a begins at the CAR PARK for **Halikouna Beach** (◉). Strike off east either along the beach or on the parallel track. When you reach the CANAL joining the so-called 'lake' to the sea, cross the FOOTBRIDGE (❶; **55min**). Then follow the sandy path into scrub. The path veers towards the lagoon and follows it for five minutes. Then it swings right, back into the scrub (take care not to continue along the side of the lagoon). Soon a narrow track comes underfoot. Emerging from the scrub, climb over the dunes, meandering through clumps of juniper and overlooking a landscape very unlike the olive-clad hills of the rest of Corfu: a lagoon trimmed in sedge and a countryside sparingly sprinkled with cottages. When the route comes back to the SEA, head left to **Issos Beach**. Go left inland through the CAR

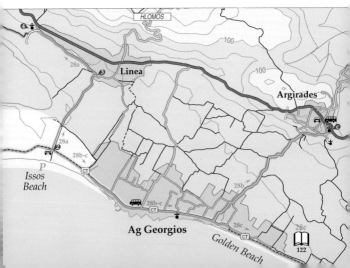

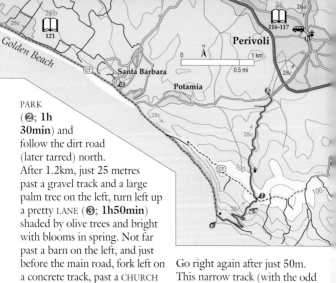

PARK
(❷; **1h 30min**) and
follow the dirt road
(later tarred) north.
After 1.2km, just 25 metres
past a gravel track and a large
palm tree on the left, turn left up
a pretty LANE (❸; **1h50min**)
shaded by olive trees and bright
with blooms in spring. Not far
past a barn on the left, and just
before the main road, fork left on
a concrete track, past a CHURCH
(❹) off to the right. After 150m
fork right on a narrower track
and follow this for just under
1km to a JUNCTION (❺) where
you turn right. The narrow route
heads 90° right, then snakes past
cultivated fields. Ignore turns left
and right until you come to a T-
junction facing a small QUARRY
(❻; **2h 35min**), then turn left
downhill.
After 150m, at the next
T-junction, go right, past a
HOUSE on the right. Almost at
once bear right uphill through
olive groves. After 170m, at a
junction, turn right. Go right
again 220m further on, at a
Y-junction. Then go straight
over a CROSSROADS (❼), through
holm oaks, and turn right at the
T-junction that follows immediately. Rise up to a concreted
lane and turn left (signed to
Bioporos, a restaurant). The
shade of eucalyptus trees is
welcome for a short stretch, then
you pass some LARGE GREEN
BUILDINGS off to the left (❽;
3h05min). Now ignore any
turnings right for a little over
1km, then take a faint track on
the right marked with red paint.

Go right again after just 50m.
This narrow track (with the odd
red waymark) bends left, then
right, then joins a wider route.
Turn right at a T-junction
(with a good view to Mt Ag
Mattheos), then the track bends
left, past a tiny CHURCH in a field
on the right. Past the church
ignore all turnings for almost
1km, until you reach a lane on
the left to 'VILLA ZAIRA'. Go left
here (❾; **4h**), descending in
'kinks' to a T-junction on the
north side of the lake. Go right,
then turn left afteer 350m, back
to **Halikounas Beach** (❍;
3h40min).
Walk b, for those travelling by
bus, **sets off** from the TURN-OFF
to **Gardiki Castle** (ⓐ). Follow
the road to the CASTLE (**10min**).
Just under 20 minutes later, bear
left on the road to **Mesavrisi**
(ⓑ). Reaching the beach and the
causeway of dunes at **Lake
Korission** (❍; **50min**), pick up
Walk a and follow it to **Issos
Beach** (❷; **2h20min**). Then
pick up a road and follow it
through **Ag Georgios**, passing a
CHURCH on the right. Five
minutes past the church, your
road to Argirades is signposted
to the left.

Above: the north side of Lake Korission is a complete contrast to the dunes in the south; left: Gardiki Castle

But first descend to **Golden Beach** (**3h10min**) for a break and a swim. Then follow the road to **Argirades** (**4h**). On entering the village, keep straight ahead to the CHURCH SQUARE (Ⓒ). Then turn left and, when you reach the main road, follow it uphill for 100m. The BUS STOP is in front of the first large olive tree on the right.

Walk c — also recommended for those travelling by bus — heads even further east. Follow WALK B above to **Golden Beach** (**3h10min**). Head east along the beach, sometimes scrambling over rocks. After 50 minutes you pass the holiday village of **Santa Barbara** (Ⓖ; **4h**). Further along

this relatively-deserted coast, you round a rocky PROMONTORY (Ⓔ; **4h45min**), a sheltered swimming spot with a number of small fishing boats. Head over to the small BRICK FISHERMEN'S SHELTER at the back of this beach and, keeping the shelter on your left, start up the track away from the beach. A couple of minutes along, you join two more tracks ascending from the beach. Climbing, you have a beautiful view of a near-deserted beach further along the coast. A steep climb brings you up to a JUNCTION at an olive grove (Ⓕ; **5h15min**).

Bear left and then immediately right, down a wider, stony track, passing a CHAPEL off to the right. Ignore any side-tracks. Join the SANTA BARBARA ROAD, and head right, crossing the BYPASS ROAD (Ⓖ). Entering **Perivoli**, keep left (due north) *not* sharp left (due west) at a junction 500m from the bypass. At the junction in front of the CHURCH BELL TOWER (Ⓗ), go left again on the main road, to the BUS STOP (**6h10min**) by the nearby cafés.

123

Walk 29: TWO CIRCUITS FROM KAVOS

Distance/time, Grade: see individual walks below
Equipment: walking boots or stout shoes, sunhat, sunglasses, suncream, long-sleeved shirt, long trousers, raingear, swimwear, picnic, plenty of water
Picnic suggestion: Moni Panagia or Kanoula Beach
Access: 🚌 to/from Kavos: motorists continue through the village and park at the side of the track to the monastery (see map; 39° 22.660'N, 20° 6.828'E). Or 🚐 to/from Kavos; journey time 1h45min. Add 15 minutes return to the walking time. Alight at the last stop in the village and walk ahead on the main road. (Do *not* fork left past the clinic with the large red cross sign.) In five minutes (after 500m) turn right at the junction. Pass the medical centre on the left, then follow the road to the left. A minute later, leave the road and turn right on the track where the walk begins.

Walk a: Moni Panagia and Kanoula Beach
Distance/time: 8km/5mi; 2h05min
Grade: ● quite easy; ups/downs of 100m/330ft, but the path past the *moni* can be very skiddy

Walk b: Moni Panagia, Kanoula Beach and Spartera
Distance/time: 10.8km/6.8mi; 3h25min
Grade: ● as Walk a, but ups/downs of about 200m/650ft. Also care is needed occasionally, clambering over rocks

At the tip of the island, in a neighbourhood of holly oaks and cypresses, lie the remains of a fortified monastery — Moni Panagia Arkoudillas. This romantic ruin sits back just out of sight of the beautifully-eroded cliffs of Cape Asprokavos. The multitude of names scrawled on the monastery walls indicates that this is probably the most walked (or cycled) track on Corfu. For the locals however, the only interest this point holds is for shooting. Don't expect to see any birds around.

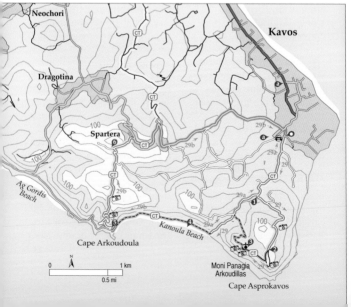

Both walks begin south of **Kavos** village, on a gravel and concrete TRACK SIGNPOSTED FOR MONI PANAGIA ('MONASTERY OF BLESSED VIRGIN MARY'; **O**). There is a **CORFU TRAIL** arrow on a pole at the left. This broad track takes you straight to the monastery. In the first few minutes ignore turn-offs to the left then the right. And within the following 10 minutes ignore two more tracks off to the right. *(Walk a will return later along the second track;* **❶** *.)*

Pass a DUMP at the right of the track (**40min**); at the FORK five minutes later, keep right (**❷**). You rise in the shade of a pretty oak wood, one of the few surviving on the island. Vines hang from the trees. But unfortunately there's another DUMP to pass, this one at the left of the track. Approaching the monastery, the track runs along the clifftops, which are hidden by vegetation. There are superb views along the dazzling white cliffs. *(If you scramble up to the edge of the cliff for a better view, do so with the utmost care! These cliffs crumble away easily!)*

Five minutes from the fork, **Moni Panagia** (**❸**; **50min**) suddenly appears, quite close to the cliff-top, in a clump of cypress trees below the track. Inside the walls are two chapels, both now ruined. Remains of stairways and walls add to the charm of the site, the more so in spring and autumn when speckled with wild flowers. Take the path on the far side of the track, into the trees. It's overgrown and involves a lot of bending and ducking, but this short foray only takes two minutes. Fork right after 20-

25m/yds; the path becomes clearer and follows the edge of the cliff, revealing a spectacular view over Kanoula Beach, which you will visit later.

Return to the *moni* and follow the path as it winds down through this enchanting forest, where the olive groves are being swallowed up by kermes oaks. Minutes downhill, the track ends at a T-junction with a path (the path to the right is so overgrown you may not see it). Head *left* for the beach: shove your way through scrub — the path is always clear. Five minutes down, cross a stream bed, then scramble up through scrub to a CONCRETE ROAD (**1h20min**) and turn left immediately. Five minutes later you're on deserted **Kanoula Beach** (**❹**; **1h25min**).

Walk a: After a break on the beach, retrace your steps up the concrete road to the beach keeping right uphill at the fork. A little over five minutes up, rejoin your outward track to the monastery, and turn left, back to the JUNCTION originally passed in the first quarter hour of the walk (**❶**). From here retrace your steps to the start of the walk at the CORFU TRAIL ARROW (**O**; **2h05min**).

Walk b continues along the broad sweep of the bay, climbing over an outcrop of rock and heading towards the cape. Amongst the seashore rocks, you come across rock samphire (*Crithmum maritimum*), a strange-smelling plant with blue-to-green fleshy leaves. Around 25 minutes along the beach, you come to a track, which leaves the beach from the far end. Follow this steeply uphill, with fine views back over Kanula Beach.

Ignore turnings left and right. After a good 1.6km you come to a T-junction, where you turn right. Then, after about 300m, turn right on the country road linking Kavos and Neochori. In a few minutes you reach the small village of **Spartera**. Follow the main road round to the right and continue for just over 2km, to a T-junction. Turn right here, back to your car at the CORFU TRAIL ARROW (**3h25min**). Or, if you came by bus, turn left and retrace your steps back to the **Kavos BUS STOP** (**3h40min**).

Moni Panagia Arkoudillas. This photograph was taken several years ago, when there were still bells in the belfry. A out-and-back walk to this monastery is highly recommended for everyone, and would round off Car tour 4 perfectly.

Walk 30: THE SALT PANS OF LEFKIMMI

See photos on pages 28-29, 30
Distance/time: 9km/5.6mi; 2h25min
Grade: ● a flat, very easy circuit; *almost no shade*
Equipment: trainers, sun

protection, picnic, water,
Picnic suggestion: the harbour
Access: 🚗 or Kavos 🚌 (journey 1h20min) to/from Lefkimmi; park/alight at the bridge at Potami (39° 25.276'N, 20° 4.745'E).

For centuries salt was extracted here by the Venetians, and in fact production only ceased as recently as 1988. Nowadays this area is better known for wildlife, and bird-watchers will not be disappointed — you can expect to see both native and migratory birds, including everyone's favourite — flamingoes. Salt-resistant plants like sea lavender thrive here, too.

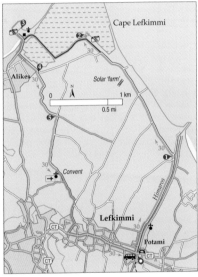

The track curves left now, and after 500m you can follow the hard-packed crusty track to the right across the pans. On the far side you meet a road behind a large stone building that was once a SALT WAREHOUSE. Walk out to the HARBOUR (❸; **1h10min**), a good, if shadeless, picnic spot (there *is* some shade below at **Alikes Beach**). Returning from the harbour, take the first road on the left. At a Y-FORK (❹) after 350m, go right. This lane ambles crookedly along for a little under 1km, to a CROSSROADS (❺) in the midst of olive groves and shady trees, where you turn right. This part of the walk, so different from the stark beauty of the salt pans, is a delight of greenery. You emerge on tarmac near a CONVENT and CEMETERY on the right. Some 350m past here, turn right at a T-junction. Then go left on the main road in **Lefkimmi**, back to the BRIDGE at **Potami** (❶; **2h15min**).

Start the walk at the BRIDGE at **Potami** (❶): head seawards along the lane on the west side of the river. After about 1km you reach a pretty little inland HARBOUR (❶). Take the second lane to the left here, then ignore lanes joining from the left after 500m and just under 1km. You pass a very modest SOLAR 'FARM' before the lane curves left. Leave the lane here, keeping ahead on a narrow track beside the SALT PANS and passing a decrepit old PUMPING STATION (❷).

BUS TIMETABLES

Note that these timetables were valid during the peak season at press date.
On either side of summer they may vary, cuts being made in mid-
September and October — when there may be only a skeleton service
until May. Or there may be more frequent services than those shown
here, which were taken from the relevant websites (see below) just
before press date. It is always worth checking to see if more — or fewer!
— buses are running; changes to services are common. *For all buses
except those with a frequent service, **check and recheck both departure and
return times first, on the web, and secondly, at the bus station**.* (Both
stations have timetables posted on site.)

All buses are run by KTEL, but buses depart from two different
stations, which I have referred to as Station 1 and Station 2.

'**Station 1**' is the terminal at San Rocco Square/Platia Georgiou
Theotoki (**blue suburban buses** for the nearby resorts both north and
south of Corfu Town, ie Dasia, Potamos, Benitses, etc). Their **website**
for up-to-the-minute timetables and and excellent route maps showing
all bus stops is **astikoktelkerkyras.gr**; tel. 26610 39858/32158.
Tickets must be bought in advance, from a bus company kiosk in the
square or a nearby shop.

'**Station 2**' is a very modern new station near the airport and Lidl.
It's about a 15-minute walk from San Rocco Square, southwest down
Dimoulitsa, or you can take a blue No 15 bus which stops there. These
green 'intercity' buses go to all other destinations on the island. Their
website, **greenbuses.gr**, has up-to-the-minute timetables and excellent
route maps showing all bus stops (as well as the exact location of their
new station). For customer service you can also call 26610 28900.
When catching a bus from Station 2, always arrive 15 minutes early.
Tickets must be bought in advance at the station, and it may take you
quite some time to *find* your bus — the station is very busy, especially
in high season. Be sure to recheck return times before setting out *with
the bus conductor/driver with whom you make the outward journey.*

Acharavi (Station 2). See Timetable 9
Achilleion (Bus No 10, Station 1). Departs 07.00, 10.00, 12.00, 14.00,
    17.00, 20.00 (Mon-Sat); departs 09.00, 13.00, 17.00, 19.00
    (Sun/holidays). Returns 20 minutes later
Afionas (Station 2). See Timetable 10
Afra (Bus No 8, Station 1). Departs 07.10, 08.00, 09.00, 11.00, 12.30,
    13.15, 14.15, 15.15, 17.00, 19.10, 21.00, 22.30 (Mon-Sat); departs
    08.00, 11.00, 13.00, 15.15, 18.00, 20.00 (Sun/holidays). Returns
    20 minutes later
Ag Georgios Beach (Station 2). See Timetable 7
Ag Gordis (Station 2). See Timetable 4
Ag Ioannis (Station 2). See Timetable 5
Ag Martinos (Station 2). Departs 05.30, 13.30 (Mon-Fri only).
    Returns 06.50, 14.50 (Mon-Fri only). Journey time 1h20min
Ag Mattheos (Station 2). Departs 06.00, 11.45, 14.30, 18.15 (Mon-
    Fri); departs 06.45, 14.00 (Sat). Returns 06.45, 12.45, 15.30, 18.50
    (Mon-Fri); returns 07.30, 15.00 (Sat). Journey time 45min
Ag Pandelimon (Station 2). Departs 05.00, 14.00 (Mon-Fri only).
    Returns 06.00, 15.30 (Mon-Fri only). Journey time 1h30min
Ag Stefanos (near Arilas) (Station 2). See Timetable 8
Ag Stefanos (near Kouloura) (Station 2). See Timetable 11
Alepou (Bus No 14, Station 1). Departs 08.15, 13.50, 17.15, 20.00
    (Mon-Sat); departs 10.00, 13.50, 18.15 (Sun). Returns 20min later
Ano Garouna (Station 2). Departs 06.00, 11.45, 14.30, 18.15 (Mon-

Fri); departs 06.45, 14.00 (Sat). Returns 06.50, 12.50, 15.35, 18.55 (Mon-Fri); returns 07.35, 15.05 (Sat). Journey time 40min

Ag Ilias (Station 2). See Timetable 11

Argirades (Station 2). See Timetables 2 and 7

Arilas (Station 2). See Timetable 10

Arkadades (Station 2). See Timetable 8

Armenades (Station 2). Departs 06.30, 13.30 (Mon-Sat only). Returns 07.30, 14.30 (Mon-Sat only). Journey time 1h05min

Avliotes (Station 2). See Timetable 8

Benitses (Bus No 6, Station 1). Departs 06.45, 08.00, 09.15, 10.30, 11.45, 13.30, 14.30, 15.45, 17.00, 18.15, 19.30, 20.45, 22.00 (Mon-Sat; fewer buses Sat pm); departs 9.00, 11.00, 13.00, 15.00, 17.00, 21.00 (Sun/hols). Returns 30mins later.

Dasia (Bus No 7, Station 1). Departs from 06.30 to 22.00 every half hour (daily). Returns 30 minutes later.

Doukades turn-off (Station 2). See Timetable 1; times approximately as Paleokastritsa

Episkepsis (Station 2). Departs 05.30, 14.00 (Mon-Sat only). Returns 07.15, 15.45 (Mon-Sat only). Journey time 1h15min

Ermones (Station 2). See Timetable 6

Gastouri (Bus No 10, Station 1). As Achilleion

Gianades (Station 2). Departs 06.15, 12.00, 14.30 (Mon-Fri only). Returns 06.45, 12.45, 15.15 (Mon-Fri only). Journey time 35min

Glyfada (Station 2). See Timetable 5

Gouvia (Bus No 7, Station 1). As Dasia

Hlomos (Station 2). Departs 05.00, 14.00 (Mon-Fri only). Departs Hlomos 06.15, 15.15 (Mon-Fri only). Journey time 1h15min

Ipsos (Station 2). See Timetable 12

Kalami turn-off (Station 2). See Timetable 11

Kanoni (Bus No 2, Station 1). Departs Mon-Fri: 06.30-22.00 every 30min; Sat: 06.30-14.30 every 30min, then every hour; Sun: 09.30-21.30 every hour; corresponding returns every 30min or every hour

Karoussades (Station 2). Departs 05.45, 09.00, 11.00, 14.00 (Mon-Sat); departs 09.30 (Sun). Returns 07.00, 10.15, 12.15, 15.00, 17.00 (Mon-Sat); returns 16.00 (Sun). Journey time 1h10min

Kassiopi (Station 2). See Timetables 11, 13

Kastellani (Station 2). See Timetable 4.

Kavadades/Magoulades junction (Station 2). See Timetable 10; times as Magoulades

Kavos (Station 2). See Timetable 2

Khoroepiskopi (Station 2). See Timetable 9

Kontokali (Bus No 7, Station 1). As Dasia

Korakades (Station 2). Departs 05.00, 13.30 (Mon-Sat only). Returns 06.30, 15.00 (Mon-Sat only). Journey time 1h

Korakiana (Station 2). Departs 06.45, 08.30, 12.15, 16.00 (Mon-Sat). Returns 07.15, 09.00, 12.45, 16.30. Journey time 25min

Krini (Station 2). Departs 07.00, 14.50 (Mon-Sat only). Returns 07.05, 15.30 (Mon-Sat only). Journey time 1h

Lafki (Station 2). Departs 04.45, 14.00 (Mon-Sat only). Returns 06.55, 16.10 (Mon-Sat only). Journey time 2h10min

Lefkimmi (Station 2). See Timetable 2

Liapades (Station 2). Departs 06.45, 14.00 (Mon-Sat only). Returns 07.15, 14.00 (Mon-Sat only). Journey time 35min

Loutses (Station 2). See Timetable 11

Magoulades (Station 2). See Timetable 10. Departures also via Armenades as above

Makrades (Station 2). Departs 06.30, 16.45 (Mon-Sat only). Returns 07.00, 14.30. Journey time 50min.

Messongi (Station 2). See Timetables 2, 3

Nimfes (Station 2). Departs 05.30, 14.00 (Mon-Fri only). Returns 07.00, 15.10 (Mon-Fri only). Journey time 1h

Nissaki (Station 2). See Timetable 11

Paleochori (Station 2). Scheduling variable; check times at station

Paleokastritsa (Station 2). See Timetable 1

Pelekas (Bus No 11, Station 1). Departs 07.00, 08.30, 10.00, 12.00, 14.15, 16.00, 18.00, 21.00, 22.00 (Mon-Sat); departs 11.00, 13.00, 19.00 (Sun/holidays). Returns 30 minutes later

Perama (Bus No 6, Station 1). As No 6 Bus to Benitses (see above)

Perivoli (Station 2). See Timetable 2

Peroulades (Station 2). See Timetable 8

Porta (Station 2). Departs 06.15, 12.15 (Mon-Sat only). Returns 07.15, 14.15 (Mon-Sat only). Journey time 1h10min

Prinilas (Station 2). Departs 06.15, 13.30 (Mon-Sat only). Returns 07.15, 14.30 (Mon-Sat only). Journey time 1h

Pyrgi (Station 2). See Timetable 12

Roda (Station 2). See Timetables 9, 13

Sfakera (Station 2). Roda bus; see Timetable 9; times approximately as for Roda

Sgombou (Station 2). See Timetable 1; times approximately as for Tsavros

Sidari (Station 2). See Timetables 8, 13

Sinarades (Station 2). See Timetable 4

Sokraki (Station 2). Departs 05.00, 14.00 (Mon-Sat only). Returns 06.00, 15.30 (Mon-Sat only). Journey time 1h25min

Spartera (Station 2). Departs 05.00, 15.00 (Mon-Sat only). Returns 06.15, 16.30. Journey time 1h25min

Spartilas (Station 2). Departs 05.30, 14.00 (Mon-Sat only). Returns 08.00, 16.30 (Mon-Sat only). Journey time 40min

Stavros (Station 2). As Strongili

Strinilas (Station 2). See Lafki bus. Journey time approx. 1h30min

Strongili (Station 2). Departs 05.45, 08.30, 12.30, 15.00, 18.15 (Mon-Fri); departs 06.30, 14.00 (Sat). Departs Strongili 07.00, 09.30, 13.30, 16.00, 19.00 (Mon-Fri); 07.15, 15.30 (Sat). Journey time 1h

Tembloni (Bus No 4, Station 1). Departs 06.40, 14.30 (Mon-Sat only). Returns 06.50, 14.50

Troumpeta (Station 2). See Timetable 9

Tsavros (Station 2). See Timetable 1

Variapatades (Station 2). Departs 06.45, 13.00, 14.30, 16.30, 20.00 (Mon-Fri); departs 08.00, 14.30 (Sat). Returns 07.15, 13.30, 15.00, 17.00, 20.30 (Mon-Fri); returns 08.30, 15.00 (Sat). Journey time 35min

Vassili (Bus No 3, Station 1). Departs daily 07.30 to 20.30 every 30 minutes. Return journeys every 30 minutes

Vatos (Station 2). See Timetable 5

Vitalades (Station 2). Departs 05.45 (Mon-Sat only). Returns 07.15 (Mon-Sat only). Journey time 1h10min

1 Corfu • Tsavros • Paleokastritsa (also Sgombou, Doukades turn-off)

Monday to Saturday			Sundays and holidays		
Corfu	Tsavros	Paleokastritsa	Corfu	Tsavros	Paleokastritsa
08.30	08.50	09.15	10.30	10.50	11.05
09.00	09.20	09.45	12.00	12.20	12.35
10.00	10.20	10.45	16.00	16.20	16.35
11.00	11.20	11.45	18.00	18.20	18.35
12.00	12.20	12.45			
13.00	13.20	13.45			
14.15	14.35	15.00			
16.00	16.20	16.45			
16.30	16.50	17.15			
17.00	17.20	17.45			
18.00	18.20	18.45			
19.00	19.20	19.45			

RETURN BUSES

Monday to Saturday			Sundays and holidays		
Paleokastritsa	Tsavros	Corfu	Paleokastritsa	Tsavros	Corfu
09.15	09.30	09.50	11.15	11.30	11.50
09.45	10.00	10.20	12.45	13.00	13.20
10.45	11.00	11.20	16.45	17.00	17.20
11.45	12.00	12.20	18.45	19.00	19.20
12.45	13.00	13.20			
13.45	14.00	14.20			
15.00	15.15	15.35			
16.45	17.00	17.20			
17.15	17.30	17.50			
17.45	18.00	18.20			
18.45	19.00	19.20			
19.45	20.00	20.20			

2 Corfu • Messongi • Argirades • Perivoli • Lefkimmi • Kavos

Daily (but only one bus on Sundays)

Corfu	Messongi	Argirades	Perivoli	Lefkimmi	Kavos
05.00+*	05.35+*	05.50+*	06.05+*	06.20+*	06.40+*
06.15*	06.50*	07.05*	07.20*	07.35*	07.55*
08.15+*	08.50+*	09.05+*	09.20+*	09.35+*	09.55+*
09.30‡•	10.05‡•	10.20‡•	10.35‡•	10.50‡•	11.10‡•
10.00+*	10.35+*	10.50+*	11.05+*	11.20+*	11.40+*
11.30*	12.05*	12.20*	12.35*	12.50*	13.10*
12.45+*	13.20+*	13.35+*	13.50+*	14.05+*	14.25+*
14.00*	14.35*	14.50*	15.05*	15.20*	15.40*
15.30*	16.05*	16.20*	16.35*	16.50*	17.10*
17.45*	18.20*	18.35*	18.50*	19.05*	19.25*
20.30*	21.05*	21.20*	21.35*	21.50*	22.10*

RETURN BUSES

Kavos	Lefkimmi	Perivoli	Argirades	Messongi	Corfu
06.15+*	06.35+*	06.50+*	07.05+*	07.20+*	07.55+*
07.45*	08.05*	08.20*	08.25*	08.50*	09.25*
09.45+*	10.05+*	10.20+*	10.25+*	10.50+*	11.25+*
11.00‡•	11.20‡•	11.35‡•	11.50‡•	12.05‡•	12.40‡•
11.30+*	11.50+*	12.05+*	12.20+*	13.35+*	14.10+*
13.00*	13.20*	13.35*	13.50*	14.05ˣ	14.40*
14.15+*	14.35+*	14.50+*	15.05+*	15.20+*	15.55+*
15.30*	15.50*	16.05*	16.20*	16.35*	17.10*
17.00*	17.20*	17.35*	17.50*	18.05*	18.40*
19.00*	19.20*	19.35*	19.50*	20.05*	20.40*
22.00	22.20	22.35	22.50	23.05	23.40

+not Saturdays; *not Sundays; • only Sundays; ‡not Monday-Friday

3 Corfu • Benitses • Messongi

		Monday to Saturday			
Corfu	Benitses	Messongi	Messongi	Benitses	Corfu
08.15	08.40	08.55	07.00	07.15	07.40
09.00	09.25	09.40	07.20*	07.35*	08.00*
10.00**	10.25**	10.40**	08.45	09.00	09.25
11.00*	11.25*	11.40*	09.50**	10.05**	10.30**
11.30	11.55	12.10	10.20**	10.35**	11.00**
12.45	13.10	13.25	11.45*	12.00*	12.25*
14.00	14.25	14.40	12.15**	12.30**	12.55**
14.30**	14.55**	15.10**	13.15	13.30	13.55
15.30	15.55	16.10	14.30*	14.45**	15.10**
16.30	16.55	17.10	16.00	16.15	16.40
17.45	18.10	18.25	17.15	17.30	17.55
19.00	19.25	19.40	18.00	18.15	18.40
20.30	20.55	21.10	19.45**	20.00**	20.25**
21.30**	21.55**	22.10**	21.45	22.00	22.25

*Saturdays only; **not Saturdays

		Sundays and holidays			
09.30	09.55	10.15	10.15	10.30	10.55
12.00	12.25	12.40	11.45	12.00	12.25
15.30	15.55	16.10	16.45	17.00	17.25
17.00	17.25	17.40	17.45	18.00	18.25
20.30	20.55	21.10	21.45	22.00	22.25

4 Corfu • Sinarades (via Kastellani) • Ag Gordis

		Monday to Saturday			
Corfu	Sinarades	Ag Gordis	Ag Gordis	Sinarades	Corfu
08.15	08.45	08.55	09.00	09.10	09.40
09.15	09.45	09.55	10.00	10.10	10.40
11.00*	11.30*	11.35*	11.45*	11.55*	12.25*
13.00	13.30	13.35	13.45	13.55	14.25
14.45	15.15	15.25	15.15	15.25	15.55
17.30	18.00	18.10	18.15	18.25	19.05
20.00	20.30	20.40	21.15	21.25	22.05

		Sundays and holidays			
11.30	12.00	12.10	12.15§	12.25§	12.55§
17.30	18.00	18.10	18.15§	18.25§	18.55§

*Not Saturdays

5 Corfu • Vatos (via Ag Ioannis) • Glyfada

	Monday to Friday			*Saturdays*	
Corfu	Vatos	Glyfada	Corfu	Vatos	Glyfada
06.30	07.00	07.10	08.30	09.00	09.10
09.00	09.30	09.40	14.00	14.30	14.40
12.00	12.30	12.40			
14.30	15.00	15.10		*Sun/holidays*	
16.00	16.30	16.40	Corfu	Vatos	Glyfada
20.30	21.00	21.10	10.00	10.30	10.40
			17.30	18.00	18.10

RETURN BUSES

	Monday to Friday			*Saturdays*	
Glyfada	Vatos	Corfu	Glyfada	Vatos	Corfu
07.00	07.10	07.40	09.00	09.10	09.40
09.30	09.40	10.10	14.45	14.05	14.25
12.30	12.40	13.10			
15.00	15.10	15.40		*Sun/holidays*	
16.55	17.05	17.35	Glyfada	Vatos	Corfu
21.15	21.25	21.55	10.30	10.40	11.10
			18.15	18.25	18.55

6 Corfu • Ermones • Corfu

Mon-Fri only: Departs Corfu 09.00, 12.00, 14.30; returns from Ermones 09.30, 12.30, 15.00; journey time 35min.

7 Corfu • Ag Georgios Beach (near Argirades)

Mon-Fri only: Departs Corfu 14.00; departs Ag Georgios 08.20; journey time about 1h

8 Corfu • Arkadades • Sidari • Peroulades • Avliotes • Ag Stefanos

Corfu	Arkadades	Sidari	Peroulades	Avliotes	Ag Stefanos
		Monday to Saturday			
05.00	05.40	06.10	06.15	06.25	06.35
08.30	09.10	09.40	09.45	09.55	10.05
11.00	11.40	12.10	—	—	—
14.00	14.40	15.10	15.15	15.25	15.35
16.00	16.40	17.10	—	—	—
		Sundays and holidays			
09.30	10.10	10.40	—	—	—
17.00	17.40	18.10	—	—	—

RETURN BUSES

Ag Stefanos	Avliotes	Peroulades	Sidari	Arkadades	Corfu
		Monday to Saturday			
06.25	06.35	06.45	07.00	07.30	08.10
10.10*	10.20*	10.30*	10.50	11.20	12.00
—	—	—	12.20	12.50	13.30
13.40*	13.50*	14.00*	14.05*	14.35*	15.15*
16.15	16.25	16.35	16.40	17.10	17.50
17.30*	17.40*	17.50*	17.55*	18.25*	19.05*
	Sundays and holidays — only one bus				
—	—	—	11.15	11.45	12.25
—	—	—	18.30	18.45	19.25

*not Saturdays

9 Corfu • Troumpeta • Khoroepiskopi • Roda • Acharavi

Corfu	Troumpeta	Khoroepiskopi	Roda	Acharavi
		Monday to Saturday		
05.00	05.30	05.40	06.00	06.15
08.30	09.00	09.10	09.30	09.45
11.00	11.30	11.40	12.00	12.15
14.00	14.30	14.40	15.00	15.15
16.00	16.30	16.40	17.00	17.15
18.30‡	19.00‡	19.10‡	19.30‡	19.45‡
20.30*	21.00*	21.10*	21.30*	21.45*
		Sundays and holidays		
09.30	10.00	10.10	10.30	10.45
17.00	17.30	17.40	18.00	18.45

RETURN BUSES

Acharavi	Roda	Khoroepiskopi	Troumpeta	Corfu
		Monday to Saturday		
07.00	07.15	07.50	08.00	08.30
09.30‡	09.45‡	10.05‡	10.15‡	10.45‡
10.20*	10.35*	10.55*	11.05*	11.35*
12.40	12.55	13.05	13.15	13.45
15.45	16.00	16.20	16.30	17.00
17.45*	18.00*	18.20*	18.30*	19.00*
19.40‡	19.55‡	20.15‡	20.25‡	20.55‡
21.45	22.00	22.20	22.30	23.00
		Sundays and holidays		
10.45	11.00	11.20	11.30	12.00
18.45	19.00	19.20	19.30	20.00

*Not Saturdays; ‡not Monday-Friday

10 Corfu • Magoulades • Afionas

			Monday to Saturday only				
Corfu	Magoulades	Afionas	Arilas	Afionas	Arilas	Magoulades	Corfu
05.00	06.05	06.20	06.40	06.25	06.40	06.50	07.55
14.00	15.05	15.20	15.40	15.40	15.55	16.06	17.10

11 Corfu • Nissaki • Kalami turn-off • Kassiopi • Ag Ilias+ • Loutses+

Journey times (approximate): Corfu to Nissaki 40min; Nissaki to Kalami turn-off 15min; Kalami turn-off to Ag Stefanos turn-off 5min; Ag Stefanos turn-off to Kassiopi 5min; Kassiopi to Ag Ilias 10min; Ag Ilias to Loutses 10min

Monday to Friday: Departs Corfu 05.15+, 08.30, 12.15, 14.30+, 17.30
Saturday: Departs Corfu 05.45, 08.30, 14.30, 17.30
Sundays and holidays: Departs Corfu 09.30, 17.00

RETURN BUSES
Monday to Friday: Departs Kassiopi 07.00, 10.15, 14.00, 16.30, 18.50
Saturday: Departs Kassiopi 07.15, 10.15, 16.30, 18.50
Sundays and holidays: Departs Kassiopi 11.15, 18.45
+On Mon, Wed, Fri *only,* these buses go on to/depart from Loutses; they depart Loutses for Corfu on Mon, Wed, Fri *only* at 06.45 and 16.00.

12 Corfu • Pyrgi/Ipsos

Monday to Saturday: Departs Corfu 05.30*, 06.00•, 08.30, 09.00, 09.30, 10.00, 11.00, 11.30, 12.15, 14.00*, 14.30, 15.30, 16.00, 16.30, 17.15, 18.30, 19.00, 20.00, 21.30; returns from Pyrgi/Ipsos 07.30, 08.00•, 09.15*, 10.00, 10.40, 11.50, 12.00, 12.50, 13.10*, 14.20*, 16.00, 17.00, 18.20, 19.30, 20.20, 21.00, 22.00
Sundays and holidays: Departs Corfu 09.30, 10.00, 11.30, 14.00, 15.30, 16.30, 18.30, 20.00; returns from Pyrgi/Ipsos 10.30, 11.00, 12.00, 14.30, 16.090, 17.00, 17.30, 17.45, 19.00, 20.30
*Not Saturdays; •Only Saturdays

13 Kassiopi • Roda • Sidari *(Summer only)*

		Monday to Saturday			
Kassiopi	Roda	Sidari	Sidari	Roda	Kassiopi
09.30	09.55	10.15	10.15	10.35	11.00
11.30	11.55	12.15	12.15	12.35	13.00
14.30	14.55	15.15	15.15	15.35	16.00
16.00	16.25	16.45	16.45	17.05	17.30
		Sundays and holidays			
Kassiopi	Roda	Sidari	Sidari	Roda	Kassiopi
11.15	11.40	12.00	10.30	10.50	11.15
16.30	16.55	17.15	16.00	16.20	16.45

● Index

Geographical names comprise the only entries in this Index. For other entries, see Contents, page 3. **Bold type** indicates a photograph; *italic* type a map (*TM* refers to the large-scale *walking map* on the reverse of the touring map). See separate index on page 128 for bus destinations and timetables. The accent ´ indicates the syllable to be stressed.

135